From France to the Farm

Blending Generational Favorites with French Flair

with
Parisienne FARMGIRL

From France to the Farm with Parisienne Farmgirl, Blending Generational Favorites with French Flair.
Copyright 2015 by Angela J. Reed.

All rights reserved.

All photographs by Angela J. Reed except the front and back cover and photos on pages 3, 13, 16, 26, 48, 56 upper right, 63 right, 72 upper left, 82 upper right, 110, 111, 112, 116 upper left, 117, 126, 142 bottom, bottom left and right, 157, 159, 186 and 210 taken by Jessica Gebbink of Jessica Lynn Studio. www.JessicaLynnStudio.com. Photo on page 160 by Jennifer Wilke-Schmid.

No part of this book my be used or reproduced in any manner without written permission. For information for permission to reproduce portions of this book for critical review and for any further inquiries contact Angela J. Reed at Angela@ParisienneFarmgirl.com.

Book design by Angela J. Reed

www.ParisienneFarmgirl.com

Printed in the United States of America.

ISBN-13:
978-1519652669

ISBN-10:
1519652666

With my whole heart I would like to thank my family; My husband Joel and my sweet chickens, Aidan, Amélie, Juliette, Julien and Anaïs. Thank you for being patient as I photographed food while you sat at the table famished. Thank you for all the extra dish duty time you put in and thank you for tolerating me while I stressed, "I've got to finish my cookbook," for the last fourteen months. Making food is my love language and, Lord knows, I love you all so very much. You are my *raison d'etre*.

Thank you to the three generations of amazing women: my Great Gramma Bauer, My Gramma Frey and my Mom for all the hours you spent in the garden and in the kitchen so I could find myself inspired one day to be just like you.

I have such a fondness for all my loyal blog readers who for years have begged me to write a cookbook. Your admiration and encouragement is what challenged me to take this on.

To Jessica Gebbink of Jessica Lynn Studios for coming out the the farm and taking such lovely photographs. You captured the spirit of my family and our life here on Half-Way Farm beautifully. Thank you from the bottom of my heart.

And thank you, Father God, for the fertile soil and for the limitless bounty you've blessed this earth with for us to enjoy. I pray any creativity I have points back to you — the Creator of the universe.

Contents

Introduction 9

Inspiration: The French Country Pantry 13

Hors d'ouevres 17
Dried Fruit and Chèvre, Foie Gras with Sauternes, Camembert with Pesto and Garlic, The Cheese Plate, What our French Friends Serve, Green Onions and Salami

Inspiration: What our French Friends Serve 26

Vinaigrettes, Sauces & Spreads 31
Tapenade of Provence, Balsamic Vinaigrette, Lemon and Oil Dressing, Homemade Brown Sugar, Clarified Butter, Lavender Honey Butter, Red Onion Confit, Béchamel Sauce, Gorgonzola Cream Sauce and Homemade Kitchen Bouquet, Pasta Sauce, Mayonnaise

Soups 49
Tomato Vegetable, Stocks, Chicken Stock, Beef Stock, 16 Bean Soup, Cream of Wild Rice with Sage, Leek and Potato Soup, French Onion Soup

From the Potager 65
Slaw Salad, Summer Broccoli Salad, Blue Cheese and Bean Potato Salad, Farm Style Green Beans, Apples and Onions, Peas -n- Cream, Potager Pizza, Braised Leeks, Herbed Farm Potatoes Two Ways, Cauliflower Gratin, Sweet Carrots

Meats 89
Pot Roast, Pork Loin with Herbs and Scallions, Salt Crust Chicken with Rosemary, Half-Way Hamburgers, Garden Tacos, Shepherd's Pie, Parisienne Pot Pie, Roast Chicken, Smoked Salmon Crêpes with Crème Fraîche, Chicken and Noodles, Summer Steak with Herb Butter

Inspiration: On Copper 108

Eggs & The Home Dairy 133
Greek Yogurt, Crème Fraîche, Feta Cheese, Quiche, Ricotta, Mozzarella, Dressed Eggs, Fried Potato Omelet, Ambrosia, Sugared Eggs

Inspiration: On Eggs 124

Inspiration: The Simple Life 140

Inspiration: On Vintage Aprons 142

Inspiration: On Table Flowers 144

The Romance of Herbs 151
Herb Bouquet, Vegetable and Herb Pairings, Meat and Herb Pairings, Herbed Butter

All Things Farine 163
Shortcrust, Chamomile and Lavender French Toast, Cinnamon Rolls, Half-Way Burger Buns, Dinner Biscuits, Classic French Pancakes, Pizza Dough, Basic Baguettes, Amélie's Honey Wheat Bread, Homemade Pasta, Apple Ricotta Pancakes, Country Loaf

Farmhouse Patisserie 189
Brambleberries with Simple Custard, Gramma's Strawberry Shortcake, Queen of Sheba Cake, Hot Fudgy Pudding, Childhood Chocolate Cake, Hot Chocolate, Triple Berry Pie, Dutch Apple Pie

Menu

My love for creating food is nothing short of a passion, but it wasn't always that way.

As a young bride living in a townhouse I didn't know much about food. Though I had spent countless hours visiting my grandparent's farm and seeing my own mother in the kitchen, I was far removed from the kitchen history and experiences of my family.

Young and inexperienced, I didn't know the first thing about homemaking, gardening or cooking. My freezer stored pre-made lasagna, and as a couple we ate a LOT of bean burritos. I had never prepared a meat dish in my life. The thought of touching raw chicken made my spine shiver, and the idea of butchering on my own never, ever even crossed my mind. I didn't even know that was an option! In my youthful ignorance, I was terrified of food. Terrified to gain a pound, I ate a no dairy, no wheat, no chocolate diet. To set our table, I weekly purchased tons of processed food from the local health food store.

Looking back I shudder at my self-inflicted torture and foolishness. And then one day I decided to take my tiny spark of an interest in the French language and turn it into something more. I decided to go on a quest to teach myself to speak French. It wasn't long before I had the courage to get on an airplane and visit France.

For one year I saved and scraped, stuffing every spare dollar I could glean from our budget into a little envelope. I soon came to my husband and presented it to him; I had saved enough for our airfare and an affordable little hotel on the rue des Cannettes. I was twenty-five years old and little did I know my life was about to change.

It is with vivid recollection that I can hear the bongs and noises of that first flight to France. I can feel my heart pounding in my chest. We were going to Paris! It was really my first time going *anywhere* aside from my Gramma's farm.

During that year of scraping and saving, I studied the language and the city of Paris with the fervor of a maniac. We took the train in from Charles de Gaulle airport, cramming every bit of stylish clothing we could afford into our suitcases. After all, I did not want to tour the city with a fanny pack and a copy of Frommer's plastered to my face. I wanted to feel... *Parisienne*.

CHEVERNY

With pride I walked us five blocks from the metro stop to our hotel without even having to look at a map. My husband was stunned. I was beaming. We learned the ropes quickly... the carte orange, café etiquette, shady neighborhoods, flea market bargaining and how to eat like the French.

It instantly became apparent that if I was going to have ANY fun in this beautiful city, I was going to have to let go of my paranoia of food. There was no such thing as a wheat-free or dairy-free diet in the City of Light that was for sure. And so I let go... and ordered a cheese plate.

Actually the first food we ordered in France was a bowl of *soupe à l'oignon* at the Depot St. Michel near the Latin Quarter. After arriving at our hotel we promptly dropped our luggage and set off to explore. As we walked I knew we were getting close to catching a glimpse of the towers of Notre Dame. And we did. It really was incredible exploring those streets and seeing things for the first time and it held a magic that only exists on your first visit.

Paris never loses its wonder but there is something noteworthy about ones first visit.

Exhausted and full of wonder at being so close to Notre Dame, we stopped and enjoyed a bowl of soup at the Depot. It was there I joyously welcomed wheat and dairy back into my life.

The rest of the week held more memories than I can cram into this book. My first trip to a Paris flea market, my first macaron, my first crêpe, my first espresso and being invited to a party as Parisians hollered to us on our hotel balcony from their apartment balcony! Did we go? *Mai bien sûr*. And I had my first Martini and got to speak French with... real Parisians.

Coming home from that trip back to the suburbs of Chicago was one of the most depressing moments of my life. Where were all the people? (Everyone in suburbia is locked in their homes in front of the television or so it seems.) Where was the architectural beauty? And WHAT were we going to eat? We promptly bought a wedge of blue cheese, a baguette and a bottle of wine and began to plan our next trip... and our next.

The next five years held two more trips to France for us. One for ten days and another for six weeks. On the six week trip I rented an apartment and immersed myself in the city as best I could, knowing that we were ready to start our family and that it would be years before I could return. It was an incredible four weeks of solitude, journaling and exploring. Strolling markets, sampling foods, retracing the steps of a much-admired queen and visiting the memorial of a much-adored princess.

My husband joined me for the remaining two weeks, and we relished in traveling the countryside, visiting friends in the Dordogne and sipping many bottles of wine back in Paris. During the time in between those trips it became clear to me that food, *excellent*, flavorful food was a pleasure I had been denying us. It also became clear to me that my appetite for knowledge was not just limited to the French language but for a desire to make that food myself. I craved learning the basics and so I did. We even moved out of our townhouse to a big old house in a historic downtown. We remodeled everything we could with French flair including the huge new kitchen where I could hone my skills.

Life shapes us doesn't it? Our family business took a huge hit with the economy, and now with a growing family under our roof, it became apparent that I could help us make ends meet by learning even more. It was time to learn how to garden. Already a proficient perennial gardener, it was time for me to learn to grow and preserve food we could actually eat. It was something that, as a stay-at-home Momma, I could do to help out.

When my firstborn was one year old, I became obsessed with the idea of a lovely, French-styled potager or kitchen garden. I grabbed a shovel and went to work carving out a circle that soon became four charming, pie wedges; raised beds built with cobblestone and pea gravel paths. I grew zucchini, onions, chamomile, peppers, lettuces and more.

I longed for more and before long we had built an "illegal" chicken coop in our garage and smuggled eight chickens into our suburban garden.

Our daily egg gathering and all its bliss lasted for one year until the neighbors turned us in. That was the catalyst. The next day we put a for sale sign in the front yard of our beloved historic home.

During this time I found myself very curious about my Gramma and her mother, Great Gramma Bauer.

What did they know that I didn't know? Great Gramma's name was often mentioned by my own mother. She showed me how to sift and measure flour like Great Gramma did. Her ways were always referred to in our little kitchen growing up.

When did these generations turn from the ways of the past like butchering hogs to buying their bacon in town and using shortening instead of lard? When did the ease of store bought canned goods outweigh labor of love in putting up the harvest of the garden in the root cellar? It was the old ways that I set out to learn, and once again I found myself on another journey with an insatiable appetite.

We now reside on "Half-Way Farm" *la Ferme a Mi-Chemin*. Our little rental farm. A place to practice our homesteading skills. We've learned to raise and butcher chickens and rabbits. We have a little goat herd and have learned animal husbandry and milking, seed starting, onion braiding and bee keeping. I've learned to make a variety of breads and tinkered with our outdoor bread oven. I've even learned some basic cheese making. It's all part of our master plan as we save for "the big one," our big family dream farm where our children can finish out their childhoods complete with dairy cow, orchards and every bucolic experience a child should have.

It is my hope that this book inspires the young bride who hasn't a clue about the ways of a kitchen to grow an herb, slice up some butter and get to work. It's also my hope that this book invigorates the seasoned housewife to try something new, to chase after her dreams, be it creating the perfect baguette or pulling up roots and trying something totally different with her life or the life of her family.

This book is a total homespun labor of love. Anything you see in this book was photographed moments before being served to my hungry family, always with a baby on my hip. These pages are a culmination of the last twenty years of my life, in the kitchen and in the garden and from France to the Farm.

I pray you enjoy it.

Angela, Parisienne **FARMGIRL**

The French Country Pantry

From France to the Farm • 13

Menu

The French Country Pantry

To make quality, delicious food you must start with quality, flavorful ingredients. There are certain foodstuffs that if you have them on hand, there is almost always a meal that can be made from scratch. The recipes in this book are for the most part, nothing extravagant; in fact, they are the basics that I build my families menus around with some drama thrown in here and there. While most of them may seem simple, even quaint, they pack a flavorful punch. Eating is one of the most basic joys of life, and as often as you can, you should sit down to a fabulous, delicious meal. At *least* once a day. Consider that for a moment. Life is full of stress, busyness and responsibilities. Why not reward yourself with incredible food at least once every twenty-four hours? So build up your pantry with incredible, healthy, decadent, flavorful items and watch dinner table come to life! Here are the items I stock my pantry with and where to buy them!

Heavy Cream-
Raw or store bought if you must. Though we can't have a cow on this property, we will on our next. Thankfully we are blessed to have a local source for raw milk and seeing that cream rise to the top is a weekly joy! Heavy cream is a staple for soups, homemade dairy products, desserts and more. And you deserve a little in your 3:00 p.m. cup of coffee!

Farm fresh eggs-
If you aren't inclined to raise your own chickens then find someone else who is and buy your eggs from them. Those eggs you are buying at the store are months old and farm fresh eggs have firm, brightly colored yolks that will bring a smile to your face.

Fresh and dried herbs-
Finding dried herbs is easy enough, and fresh herbs are just as easy to grow in pots on your windowsill. You simply must have them on hand for the sheer joy of the aroma they release as they are cut under your knife. In addition to my herb garden, I keep Herbes de Provence on hand for maximum flavor.

Quality flour-
Known as *farine* in French, finding a flour that works for you and your family is so important. I personally love to order my flour from War Eagle Mill. I buy mine organic, unbleached and unbromated. I do keep a supply and variety of wheat kernels on hand but I save them for those days where I have the time to grind it and can truly fuss over the process. Never, ever feed your family enriched flour if you can help it. Enriched flour should not be used because iron has been added to it. It is a metallic iron and not a nutrient iron. Being a metallic iron, it is not bioavailabile for the human body and was never meant to be consumed. Also, enriched flour is not absorbed as a grain but as a starch.

Extra Virgin Olive Oil-
Extra virgin olive oil, with its distinctive taste, is a staple for any cook, aspiring or pro. EVOO is extracted using natural methods and contains vitamins E and K. Once a year we stock up on our favorites at The Oilerie in Fish Creek, Wisconsin.

Quality Balsamic Vinegar-
Here's a simple rule that will take you far: buy the best balsamic vinegar that your income allows. It's used for salad dressings, glazes, deserts and the finest can be sipped in a cordial glass. I stock my pantry with balsamic vinegar that's been aged 25 years, again from The Oilerie.

Dried Beans-
Split pea, lentils, navy beans and more. An inventory of dried beans is excellent for soups, ragu and cassoulet.

Onions-
I grow a little over one thousand onions each year because I use at least a couple a day. Braided, they hang in my pantry and even more in my cellar, and between the braids and onions fresh out of the garden we stay "in onion" all year long. Onions are a necessity. Enough said.

Garlic-
In my kitchen there is a motto, "When in doubt, add more garlic." Sweet, savory and powerful this amazing member of the onion family can be purchased at your local farmers market or home grown, dried and braided like onions.

Pure, Unrefined Sea Salt-
Sea salt provides a slightly higher mineral content than regular table salt. Our favorite is the gray sea salt that is sourced off the coast of Brittany. Harvested by hand using traditional Celtic methods, we prefer its texture and feel that it adds additional flavor to our food. I purchase mine through Williams Sonoma.

Peppercorns-
Freshly-ground, rainbow peppercorns are always on our table, ready for use.

Yeast-
With flour, salt and yeast you are always a couple hours away from something delicious. Red Star yeast is readily available, but I also recommend SAF. Upon opening, store your yeast in an airtight jar in the refrigerator.

Wine-
There are three wines (minimum) that you should stock in your French Country Pantry; a dry white for cooking, a quality red for drinking (we prefer Bordeaux) and a sweet dessert wine for preparing desserts and enjoying them.

A variety of pork-
By keeping a variety of pork on hand you can prepare a myriad of dishes. Bacon and pancetta will compliment your eggs or (dried) bean dishes. Chops and loin can be complimented with seasonal fruits and herbs. I find pork extremely useful to always have on hand.

Let's dispense with one more little necessity. Though I won't always use descriptive words like "home-grown," "farm raised" or "organic" in this book, you can rest assured that it is implied. As much as it is in your ability to do so, I encourage you to eat organic, raise your own food or find a farmer who will raise it for you.

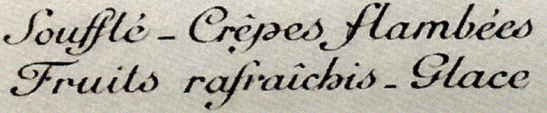 

Dried Fruit and Chèvre

-fruits secs au chèvre

Though the French serve their cheese after dinner but before dessert (which is served *before* coffee), this cheese dish can be served as an appetizer at any party or of course as a colorful addition to your dinner's cheese course.

You will need:
1 chèvre log or two cups of homemade chèvre
½ cup of raisins (I use a tri-color variety)
½ cup of cranberries
½ cup of dried blueberries
¼ cup of extra virgin olive oil
½ cup of honey, more to taste if desired
1–2 tablespoon of fresh thyme

Take care to remove your cheese from the refrigerator thirty minutes before beginning to soften it. Mince the garlic in a food processor to peppercorn size. Add the fruit and pulse to your desired size and then add the olive oil. Arrange the chèvre log on serving plate or platter and the fruit mixture on top of the cheese. Drizzle the honey over the top and sprinkle with thyme. Serve with baguette slices or crackers.

Serves 4–6

Parisienne Farmgirl hint:
For extra fun, roast a handful of pine nuts in a dry skillet and sprinkle them over the cheese just before serving.

Foie Gras Mousse with Sauternes
-mousse de foie gras au sauternes

All throughout the French countryside are farmer's wives who have perfected the art of raising *foie gras*. They share with friends, family and sell to the local markets. Their timeless skill is both controversial and appreciated all over the world.

Foie gras, or goose liver, is quite simply one of my most favorite foods, and here in the States it can be ordered fresh, frozen or in convenient little tins or uncooked for those ready to make their own.

Foie gras can be sautéed and served on a salad or with a choice cut of meat but this way is my favorite: with a little fig spread and a glass of Sauternes. If you ever find yourself at a French restaurant and wanting to impress your waiter order the *foie gras* hors d'oeuvre and a glass of Sauternes. Eyebrows will raise in respect and it will be thought that you clearly know what you are doing.

You will need:
Quality foie gras (If goose liver is unavailable duck liver will do in a pinch. I purchase mine from Trois Petits Cochons or d'Artagnan)
Toast points
Figs or fig jam
Fresh ground pepper
Fresh ground sea salt
A beautiful glass of Sauternes

Toast your bread. Spread your *mousse de foie gras* and enjoy one of the most simple and delicious dishes on the planet.

Oh, I forgot. This is an hors d'oeuvre. You may have to share.

Weary after a long day of traveling from Paris to Bordeaux, Joel and I stumbled down the tiny streets of St. Emilion looking for the perfect place to eat. The restaurant we chose was jam packed but with much apology the staff offered to seat us in the wine cellar. They were regretful but we were thrilled and we dined surrounded by crates of wine, stone walls and a gravel floor. I enjoyed seared foie gras with a glass of Moulin de Saint George. That meal is one of my favorite food memories of all time.

Camembert with Pesto and Garlic

-camembert au pesto et à l'ail

I'll confess. I've been to a nude beach. Oops. Thankfully I had this delicious dish to distract me from the older gentlemen that should *not* have been there, lest I be traumatized for life.

If you are ever in Saint Martin at Orient Bay Beach there is a little beach-side bar where you can hide and order this. I came right home from that tropical paradise and recreated it. Thankfully it reminds us of white sands and salty sea air and not other things. *Ahem!*

Serves 4

You will need:
1 small round or large wedge of Camembert cheese
1–2 heads of garlic, separated and peeled
½ cup of pesto

Peel the garlic and toss the cloves in olive oil so that each piece is coated. In an oven-proof bowl place your round or wedge of Camembert, spread the pesto on top and arrange the garlic on and around.
Broil until garlic begins to brown.

Serve with crackers or sliced baguette.

From France to the Farm • 23

The Cheese Plate

-le plateau de fromage

The cheese plate.
Oh! How I love thee.

This elegant part of entertaining is typically served after the meal but before the dessert during the traditional French dinner, however, stateside we are more likely to serve a cheese plate at a party or as a decedent hors d'oeuvre.

The cheese plate can be served with fruit and crusty bread but variety is what will make your cheese plate appealing to all.

On my cheese plate I try to offer an assortment of textures and flavors made from a variety of milks. It is amusing to me to watch people enjoy the cheese plate; the bravery someone summons when trying a blue cheese for the first time and the decedent guilt they inflict upon themselves as they slather the creamy goodness on a crusty piece of bread. By serving the cheese plate after the meal, before the dessert like the French do, you are giving these beautiful cheeses the spotlight they deserve.

I think it is always lovely to offer a standard double crème Brie. Brie is a soft ripened cheese named after the region in France from which it comes. It's buttery and can be runny. Its flavor is nutty and mild and a favorite of many. I love a fine slice of Brie with a wedge of Granny Smith apple.

Every cheese plate should have a blue cheese and my favorite is a German cheese called Cambozola. The blend of a triple crème French soft ripened cheese and an Italian Gorgonzola. It's made with the same *Penicillium roqueforti* mold that is used to make cheese like Roquefort and Stilton. Both could be used to add a blue cheese to your cheese plate, but Cambozola is our favorite.

To give additional variety be sure to offer a variety of textures. You can do this by offering a pressed cheese like Comté. Made in eastern France in the Franche-Comté region. Nutty and versatile this cheese has PDO status (Protected Designation of Origin) meaning that to be called Comté it can only come from a certain area in France and strict methods must be followed. Wheels of this cheese must be aged for a minimum of four months, and as it ages the flavors become more pronounced. Unique crystals in aged Comté are a sign of maturity and quality. Other pressed cheeses you might want to try include the fabulous Morbier (another favorite around here) and Beaufort.

Last but not least, every cheese plate, even the simplest, should include a goat cheese, and I can't resist a classic chèvre. In fact, we make our own all the time, as it is difficult to find in stores in our area. Chèvre is a soft, rindless cheese with an earthy quality that sets it apart from the cow's milk cheeses on your cheese plate. Chèvre comes in logs, pyramids and rounds.

What our French Friends Serve

Before we began our family, we had quite a collection of French friends that lived near us. We were invited to join in their monthly tradition of a decadent pot-lock. A chance for all of them to speak their lovely language for an entire evening.

Many of these friends have since moved across the country or even returned to France. With some, we have lost contact all together and with others we still stay in touch, hoping to visit them on their own turf someday.

These soirées are fond, fond memories for me. Though I often found myself hanging on for dear life with their rapid-fire French, they we always generous with their explanations, and it did my humble language skills a service that I still benefit from to this day.

We noticed that the same things were offered on the coffee table before every meal no matter who was hosting. Maybe it's just the way our little group did things, but we have adopted these customs and use them when we entertain as a way to remember those wonderful days of culture and friendship.

This is what they served...

PORTO

Yes, we call it Port but our friends called it "Porto" and my husband loves it. I find it very heavy and sweet, but it does the job of stimulating the palate. It is referred to as a fortified wine and comes from the same wine family as Sherry and Madeira. I'll leave it for my husband and take a glass of...

Champagne

Un ver du champagne?

Yes please! Champagne is my personal favorite apéritif. Brut in particular. A glass or two and you will find yourself well ready to begin an evening of dining.

Nuts

Setting out a small display of hors d'oeuvres need not be gaudy and fantastic. A small bowl of nuts on the table. Every. Time.

OLIVES

Simple. In a bowl with some toothpicks or small forks. Plain or stuffed with garlic or blue cheese; olives are a treat and give you something to eat without ruining your appetite.

CORNICHONS

Small, salty, delicious little pickles. Need I say more?

Saucisson

From the charcuterie family this is a cured, air-dried sausage similar to American's summer sausage. It is primarily pork but can be made of other meats and is flavored with garlic.

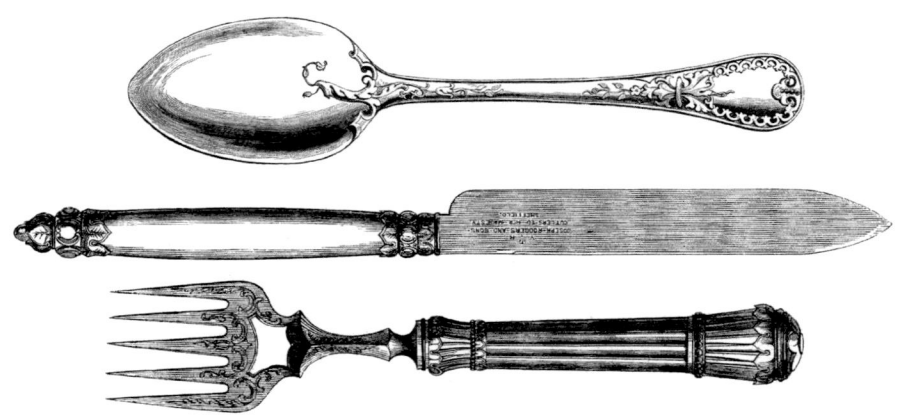

From France to the Farm

Green Onions and Salami

-oignons verts et saucisson

Five of these, a glass of wine and I'm set. That's a meal! Every single time I make these people go crazy. It's the pleasing combination of color, texture and taste. We've been making them in my family for years and they are a win-win every time. This is an excellent project for your little ones, if you are busy in the kitchen and they are dying to "help you."

You will need:
Fresh green onions
Cream cheese
Thin sliced salami

Spread a thin layer of cream cheese (homemade or store bought) on each piece of thinly cut salami and wrap it around the bottom portion of each green onion. Take care to remove the bottom, root portion of the onion first. Arrange in a pleasing fashion and enjoy.

Vinaigrettes, Sauces and Spreads

Tapenade of Provence
-tapenade Provençale

Our favorite French bistro serves tapenade with crusty bread while you wait for your meal. I dare say that some times I wish I hadn't ordered anything off the menu, for tapenade is a wonderful thing. One day I lined my counter top with a food processor and every ingredient I thought I tasted at the restaurant the night before... *et voilà!*

You will need:
4 cups of green olives (pimentos do not need to be removed)
1 ½ cups of Greek olives
3 large carrots, orange or yellow, peeled
½ cup of lemon juice
½ cup of canola or olive oil
2 teaspoons of Italian seasonings
2 tablespoons of white wine mustard
Sea salt to taste

Using a food processor chop the carrots into ½ inch pieces. Add the rest of the ingredients and pulse chop, scraping the sides down as needed.

Slather onto a fresh or toasted baguette and enjoy. Refrigerate any leftovers. This will keep in the refrigerator for one week.

You may also like to experiment by adding capers, red peppers, onion and tomato. For an extra salty taste try adding an anchovy. Serves enough for a large party!

Makes about six cups.

Balsamic Vinaigrette

-vinaigrette balsamique

This is my *vinaigrette classique*. I use it on salads and I love to have a little on the side of a slice of quiche and even pizza.

You will need:
1 cup of quality balsamic vinegar (For fabulous, rich results I use vinegar that is aged 25 years. See page 15.)
1 ½ cups of extra virgin olive oil
1 tablespoon of white wine mustard
1 crushed garlic clove (for best results press through a garlic press)
2 tablespoons of lemon juice
Finely crushed Herbes de Provence to taste
Sea salt and ground pepper to taste

Combine everything except the olive oil in a mason jar or dressing bottle, cover with the lid and mix well. Remove the lid and add a little olive oil. Replace the lid and shake. Continue until you have added all the olive oil. For a lighter taste add extra lemon juice. Store in a glass jar or bottle. Lasts for up to one month in the fridge.

Makes about 2 ½ cups.

Lemon and Oil Dressing
-vinaigrette à l'huile de citron et d'olive

I came home from Paris absolutely desperate to imitate the taste I had on so many salads. This is what I came up with. This dressing is light and citrusy and excellent on salads such as an endive with blue cheese.

You will need:
½ cup of extra virgin olive oil
¼ cup of quality lemon juice or fresh squeezed lemon juice
1 tablespoon of lemon zest
1 tablespoon of Dijon mustard
Sea salt to taste

Combine ingredients in a canning jar and shake. Can be stored in the refrigerator for up to one week. Makes just under two cups.

Homemade Brown Sugar
-sucre roux fait maison

You will need:
1 cup of sugar
2 tablespoons of black strap molasses

Mix well and enjoy.

Homemade brown sugar is another fine example of something simple that you can make yourself, and once you do, you'll never go back to store bought. I suppose you could say this really doesn't need to be in a cookbook, but I beg to differ. Homemade brown sugar brings a serious depth to your sweets, sauces, meat dishes and more that store bought cannot. It will take your dark chocolate cakes to the next level. It's all about the molasses in our house. Our goats love molasses, too! The recipe can, of course, be multiplied to suit your needs but is best made fresh as needed.

Makes a little more than one cup.

Clarified Butter Sauce
-sauce clarifiée au beurre

Clarified butter is the base of many basic, French sauces. By removing the impurities, milk solids and water from the butter you are clarifying it, leaving behind only pure butterfat. Choose a high quality, Irish butter or homemade butter for excellent results.

You will need:
8 ounces of quality, unsalted butter
(You will end up with about 6 ounces of clarified butter)

Over a very low flame, heat your butter in a heavy-duty saucepan. Once it has melted let it simmer a bit and the foam will rise to the top. The butter may spritz, so use caution. Once it has stopped spritzing and the foam is no longer rising, skim off what you can with a spoon.

Line a small bowl with a fine mesh strainer and then multiple layers of cheesecloth and carefully pour the butter into the bowl.

Using caution, pour the butter into your container of choice. I use a mason jar. Clarified butter can be stored in the refrigerator or freezer for up to six months.

When you go to use your clarified butter remember that you are working with pure butterfat that now has a smoke point of 400–450 degrees as compared with regular butter who's smoke point is 350 degrees.

You can use clarified butter like you would any other butter, but it really does its thing in dishes where you are meant to taste the butter like roasted, farm fresh vegetables, steaks and fish.

Makes six ounces.

Lavender Honey Butter
-beurre de miel de lavande

The only verb you should apply to this butter is "slather." Slather it across your favorite English muffin or dinner biscuit. The creamy, warm goodness of this butter calls for a piping hot cup of coffee or tea and "more please."

You will need:
16 ounces of unsalted butter
2 tablespoons of dried, edible lavender buds
6 tablespoons of honey

Whiz all the ingredients in a food processor until whipped. You may also like to crush the lavender with your mortar and pestle before beginning.

Store in a jar in the refrigerator. Remove to bring the butter to room temperature thirty minutes before serving.

Makes about one pint.

Red Onion Confit
-confiture d'oignons rouges

A confiture of red onion will revolutionize the most traditional meat and fish dishes.

You will need:
1 tablespoon minced garlic
¼ cup minced shallot
½ teaspoon dried thyme, crumbled
1 tablespoon olive oil
2 ½ cups thinly sliced red onion
½ cup grenadine
1 cup of sugar
3 tablespoons of balsamic vinegar
2 tablespoons minced fresh parsley leaves

Heat the oil and add minced onion and shallots cooking for about five minutes.

Add the balsamic vinegar and grenadine and bring them to a boil. Add the sugar and herbs and continue to boil for ten more minutes. Add salt and pepper to taste. Store in a jar in the refrigerator. Chill overnight before serving with any meat or fish dish.

Makes about one pint.

Flower Pepper
-poivre de fleurs

It is so important for me to search out ways to make every day life more beautiful, and it may sound crazy but this simple recipe does that for me. The entire process pleases me from planting the seeds to enjoying the fresh flowers during the summer. My sweet girls and I love to harvest the blossoms daily. The fragrance of the peppercorns when you dump them into the ball jar and shake them into the lemon zest is heady. I promise if you make this Flower Pepper you'll never use regular pepper again. Look at it! It's gorgeous! I love seeing it on my counter. We use ours every day on eggs, salads, meat dishes and you will too!

You will need:
½ cup calendula
¼ cup lavender buds
½ cup nasturtiums
3 tablespoons of lemon zest
1 cup peppercorns

You will also need dried lemon zest and rainbow peppercorns.

Combine everything to taste in a ball jar, shake and pour into a pepper grinder.

Béchamel Sauce

-sauce béchamel

Béchamel sauce is a classic French sauce that can be paired with your favorite farm food like roast chicken and vegetables from the garden like asparagus and spinach. My favorite use for *sauce béchamel* is in Cauliflower Gratin and it is the base for Parisienne Pot Pie on page 100.

For about 2 cups of sauce you will need:
4 tablespoons of butter
4 tablespoons of flour
2 cups of milk, plus a little more if your sauce becomes too thick.
1 teaspoon of sugar
½ teaspoon of salt
Fresh grated nutmeg to taste

In a heavy skillet melt the butter on low and stir in the flour. Stir for 3 minutes. This removes the pasty, flour taste. Do not allow it to brown. Continue stirring and add the remaining ingredients until the sauce thickens. Makes about 2 ½ cups.

Gorgonzola Cream Sauce

-sauce à la crème au Gorgonzola

This sauce can be served with any red meat or pork and is just as good as a unique spread or dipping sauce for your favorite hamburger. It can be made up ahead of time and frozen to have on hand for that special meal.

You will need:
2 tablespoons of butter
1 tablespoon of flour
1 cup of crème fraîche (see page 115)
½ cup of dry white wine
½ cup of chicken stock
1 cup of Gorgonzola cheese

Melt the butter but do not let it brown. Once it has melted remove from heat and add the flour, whisking until thoroughly blended. Slowly add the crème fraîche, white wine and stock. Whisking as the mixture becomes thicker. Add Gorgonzola and blend until the mixture is smooth. Makes about 2 cups.

Homemade Kitchen Bouquet

Kitchen Bouquet is a store-bought browning sauce that has been used in the kitchens of our Gramma's and Great Gramma's since the year 1889. In fact, it was one of the products featured in America's exhibit at the Paris Exposition of that same year. My Momma swears by it for her pot roast and gravies and I, true to form, swear by making my own.

½ cup of Homemade Brown Sugar (page 35)
1 cup of water
2 tablespoons of Beef Stock (page 54)

In a small saucepan heat the brown sugar until it begins to really brown, about 7–10 minutes. Add one cup of water and stir until the sugar is dissolved. Add the beef stock, mix until blended and heat until slightly reduced. Homemade Kitchen Bouquet will store in the refrigerator in your favorite jar. Makes 1 ½ cups. Use 3–6 tablespoons to help with browning.

Pasta Sauce
-sauce pour pâtes

I have so many Italians in my family, I joke that I am Italian by default. Plus, there is the whole nose thing.

As a young wife, learning to make my own sauce was as liberating as learning how to make roast chicken. I could now make pizza, pasta and lasagna for my family, knowing exactly what they were eating. Nothing says, "I love you," like a big stockpot full of simmering sauce. At least, that's the way my children see it. I typically make up a very large batch of sauce and then freeze it, due to the effort involved.

If you're a gardener who is blessed enough to grow your own tomatoes then, by all means, make your pasta sauce with tomato sauce you've made from your garden. Sadly, here on our farm it is an uphill battle to grow tomatoes due to the black walnut trees. They release a chemical into the soil making it toxic for tomatoes, peppers, cucumbers and more. We grow our tomatoes in raised beds with soil we have brought it and so our space is limited, and I can never quite grow enough to make a significant amount my own tomato sauce. Someday.

The idea behind this sauce is free flowing, so don't be afraid to experiment with your own quantities of meat, herbs or olive oil. You won't ruin it. While the idea is much the same, every family has their own style of pasta sauce. This is ours.

By following these directions you will make one stockpot full of sauce however, it can be doubled, tripled, etc. if you would like to fill your freezer or line your pantry shelves.

You will need:
About 60 ounces of tomato sauce
1 pound of Italian pork sausage (spice level depends on your preference)
One large yellow onion
Two large handfuls of fresh Italian herbs or four tablespoons of dried herbs (oregano, basil, rosemary)
1 head of garlic
1 tablespoon of crushed red pepper
Olive oil

In a food processor or by hand mince the onions, garlic and herbs.

In a large stockpot add enough olive oil to sauté the onions, garlic and herbs. Once the onion mixture is beginning to turn golden, add the tomato sauce and stir thoroughly.

Using a sharp knife, slice the uncooked sausage and remove the casing. Over medium heat cook the sausage until it is a little more than half done.

Transfer the half-cooked sausage to the a food processor and pulse until it is ground. For extra flavor add a tablespoon or two of the sausage grease to your stockpot. Add the minced sausage to the tomato sauce and simmer on very low heat for at least three hours. Stir occasionally so the tomato sauce does not scald on the bottom of the pot. Can in a pressure cooker, freeze or serve.

Serve with any pasta or on pizza.

Mayonnaise

-mayonnaise

I was never a mayonnaise person until visiting France for the first time. It was there that I tried it with *pommes frites* that were served with my *steak au poivre*.

Coup de foudre!

In France mayonnaise often comes in toothpaste-like tubes and I loaded my suitcase with as many as would fit. Olive oil, white wine mustard and red wine vinegar give this mayonnaise an extra tang. Why not make your own classic bistro fare and enjoy some with your next steak and French fries?

You will need:
(All ingredients should be room temperature)

3 egg yolks
5 tablespoons of red wine vinegar
1 ½ –2 cups of olive oil
2 tablespoons of white wine mustard
Salt to taste
Pepper to taste

Do not attempt to make homemade mayonnaise unless you have at least ten to fifteen minutes and are feeling plenty patient. You will become more confident with each batch. The key to the proper consistency is adding the oil drop by drop.

Beat your room temperature egg yolks for a minute or two until they become thick. Drop by drop add the olive oil. You can use a hand mixer or a stand mixer with the balloon whisk attachment. I find it easiest to use my stand mixer and pour a little oil over the head of the mixer, allowing it to drip down into the bowl. The olive oil must be added drop by drop. After the mixture begins to form a heavy cream, you can increase the amount of olive oil you are adding from drop by drop into a thin stream.

Add the rest of your ingredients, adjusting to taste. Remember, this will not taste like store bought mayonnaise.

This will keep in the refrigerator for up to one week.

Makes about 1 ½ cups.

Soups

Stocks

I believe it is absolutely essential for anyone who spends time in their kitchen to know how to make their own meat and vegetable stocks. They are the primary basis for delicious soups and sauces and are called for in various pasta dishes too.

There is no comparison when it comes to the flavor of a stock that's been simmering on your stove top for eighteen hours as compared to store bought canned or boxed stock. Making your own will improve any dish where stock is required. There is also no comparison when it comes to health benefits of homemade versus store bought. Homemade stocks are void of excess sodium, MSG and a myriad of other unhealthy ingredients found in canned or boxed stocks. They can be frozen for up to a year or canned with a pressure canner for your well-stocked pantry.

It could be easily said that chicken stock is the core of my dinnertime repertoire. Knowing how to make chicken stock is useful in the making of soups, risottos, sauces and more. Not to mention the simple enjoyment that comes from flavorful, hot, mugful.

It's not just an old wives' tale. When made from scratch, stock offers the body a variety of nutrients. My children love to drink it by the mugful and its aroma fills our home with comforting goodness. The little ones beg for it as "chicken dock."

Every stock making home has their favorite way. These are ours.

Chicken Stock

-bouillon de poulet

You will need:
1–3 carcasses of yesterday's roast chicken
(I freeze mine so I have them on hand when it's stock making time!)
2 onions, quartered
1 head of garlic
1 bunch of celery with leaves
1 large or two small leeks
½ cup of apple cider vinegar
1 bunch of carrots (3–4)
1 *bouquet garni*
Cracked pepper and sea salt to taste

Fill an extra large stockpot full of water. Exact water measurements really don't matter so if this is your first time, don't panic! There is nothing that a little more time on the stove or a little more salt won't fix! Quarter the onions, and smash the garlic cloves (I don't even remove the skins if they are clean) and combine all the ingredients in the stockpot.

Simmer on low all day and before you retire for the evening, turn off the heat and after your burner has cooled off wrap a large towel around your pot, closing in the heat. Be sure your stove top has cooled off. In the morning remove the towel and return the stock to a simmer until the end of the day. I simmer mine for a total of eighteen to twenty-four hours, salting as needed. Salt is the key to pulling out the flavor of your stock so don't be afraid to use it!

When you have a lovely golden stock, strain your vegetables. If you've used a whole chicken you can save the meat for chicken and noodles (see page 104). Discard the vegetables or feed them as a treat to your chickens or rabbits.
Enjoy weeks and weeks of chicken stock for all your from-scratch recipes! Be sure to enjoy a cupful of your accomplishment and freeze the rest in sealed containers or can it with a pressure canner.

Parisienne Farmgirl hint:
The gel that appears as your stock cools is a GOOD thing! It is simply gelatin from the chicken bones and it is very nutritious! It will dissolve again upon reheating.

Beef Stock
-bouillon de boeuf

You will need:
Beef bones (with some meat still left on them)
Water
4 celery stalks
1 large onion
2 large leeks
2 Bay leaves
1 large bunch of thyme
1 head of garlic
½ teaspoon of peppercorns

Brown the meat (still attached to the bone) in a skillet with a little butter and then follow the Chicken Stock directions and enjoy!

From France to the Farm

Tomato Vegetable

-potage aux légumes de tomate

After you are done with your pot roast you have two choices; you can make gravy or you can use the broth to make this delicious soup. This is a traditional meal on my Gramma's farm. I loved this soup for as long as I can remember.

In a large stockpot or slow cooker combine the following ingredients:
7–8 cups of tomato sauce
3 cups of beef stock (see page 54)
1 cup of pearl barley
Any meat, potato and carrot leftovers for your Pot Roast (page 90)
1 cup of white corn
½ pound of green beans (fresh or frozen)
White pepper to taste
Sea salt to taste

Simmer on low, making sure it does not stick to the bottom. The soup is ready once the barely has softened. Serves 8 with leftovers. Can be frozen.

Cream of Wild Rice with Sage
-crème de zizanie à la sauge

Savory, time saving, healthy and satisfying. Here on Half-Way Farm aromas travel fast. I've been told that you can smell my bread baking and soup simmering clear down the lane. My front door opens right into the kitchen and it is a pleasure to have the fragrance of a hot soup greet our random guests, and with egg sales and people curious about the farm… we have a lot of those.

You will need:
Two quarts chicken stock, plus more if desired
1 pint of heavy cream, plus more if desired
1 ¼ cup wild rice
1 large yellow onion, finely diced
1 clove of garlic, minced
1 large branch of sage
4 tablespoons of butter
Sea salt and cracked pepper to taste

In a heavy-duty stockpot melt the butter and sauté the garlic and onion. Add the chicken stock and the branch of sage to the soup like a *bouquet garni*. You will fish it out before you serve the soup. Cook over medium low heat, allowing the rice to soften. Once it has, add the cream. You may want to add more cream or stock to reach your desired consistency. Remove the sage branch and any larger leaves that became loose and salt and pepper to taste.

Serves 6–8.

16 Bean Soup

-soupe aux seize fèves

Seven people are a lot of mouths to feed and sometimes this Mamma is just burned out. Slow Cooker to the rescue! It's so easy; it's almost a shame to give away my secret. Here's to the five-dollar meal!

You will need:
1 bag of 16-bean blend (throw away the MSG filled flavor packet)
2 garlic cloves, minced
1 medium onion, minced
3–4 quarts of chicken stock
Crème fraîche or sour cream
Olive oil to sauté
Salt to taste

Special Equipment:
Slow cooker

Rinse your beans and check them for small stones. (Yes, it DOES happen.) Put them in a slow cooker with the three quarts of the chicken stock and set it on your desired temperature. In a medium sized skillet, heat the olive oil and sauté the garlic and onion until the onion begins to turn clear. Add the onion and garlic mixture to the beans. Check the beans periodically for the need to add more stock and do so before your beans become dry. When the beans are soft, add your salt to taste and serve with a big dollop of crème fraîche or sour cream. Serves 6–8 with the occasional leftovers.

Parisienne farmgirl hint:
For variety and extra flavor, try frying up a pound of bacon and use half the grease to sauté the onion and garlic. Add the crumbled bacon to the soup when serving.

Leek and Potato Soup

-vichyssoise servie chaude

I consider us very blessed to serve this meal, because ninety-nine percent of it comes from our farm. When we sit down *à table* the delicious taste is accompanied by a sense of pride, as we remember the tiny leeks we planted in the spring (as tiny as a blade of grass when transferred from the greenhouse to the potager), the potatoes that the little girls planted and the celery that I struggled to grow. Growing celery is not my forté. Not to mention the chickens we raised which provided the stock.

This is a classic French soup and a favorite for my children. Serve cold as *Vichyssoise* or warm (as we like it). When paired with a big crusty loaf of bread and a creamy slather of butter... well, it doesn't get much better.

Serves 6–8

You will need:
4 large or 7–8 medium sized leeks
½ an onion
5 Yukon Gold potatoes
2 quarts of chicken stock
4 tablespoons of butter
One small bunch of tender celery with leaves
Salt and Pepper to taste

Remove the green ends of the leeks and wash them thoroughly as garden dirt can tend to hid in the layers. Chop them into small slices and rinse again. Mince the onion and sauté both in butter on low in a large skillet until soft. About 30 minutes.

In a large stockpot heat the chicken stock. Quarter the potatoes and add all the vegetables and simmer until soft.

Purée in a food processor, salt and pepper to taste and serve hot or cold.

Option: Peel the potatoes or press through a sieve before serving. We happen to like the heartiness the potato peel gives to the soup

French Onion Soup
-soupe a l'oignon gratinée

Feet throbbing, stomachs growling and spirits completely intimidated by the throngs of trendy Parisians spilling out onto the sidewalks in front of every café and pub in the Latin Quarter, all we wanted was to sit down and savor the moment. It was our first trip to Paris, and every second was to be remembered. We spotted a quiet little bistro with no bumping bass coming from inside. Only empty tables and a chalkboard menu. Fifteen years ago my French skills were not what they are today. I scanned a scribbled menu in search of *soupe à l'oignon*. The curly-Q font of the standard French handwriting throwing me off. Is that a "one" or a "seven" and how is it that they all seem to have identical handwriting? Thanks to Napoleon, I am sure. The word onion was no where to be found on this little menu, propped up against the entry way, but the place was quiet and *vide*... empty, and the patron seemed pleased to invite us in. I inquired about the soup, *S'il vous plait. Avez-vous du soupe à l'oignon* but with much regret our waiter informed me that they did not have my much-coveted onion soup. I understood, it was, after all, not on the menu and around eleven in the evening. We requested two more minutes so I could decide what to order but before those two minutes where up our waiter came back and with a gentle enthusiasm that I did not expect to encounter in our garçon (he is not to be called that of course!), he announced that they had found what they needed and could "whip me up a bowl." Ok, he didn't say it just like that but a short time later a piping hot bowl of "French Onion Soup" (as we call it Stateside) came out and to my delight, it was wonderful! Imagine my joy a few years later when I figured out how to recreate the taste from that special evening!

You will need:
1 ½ pounds of sweet or yellow onions (about 8), sliced thin
2 tablespoons of flour
4 tablespoons of butter
1 quart of chicken stock
1 cup of dry white wine
Bouquet garni
Yesterday's baguette in thin slices
½ pound of Swiss or Gruyere cheese, sliced
Sea salt and pepper to taste

In a 5-quart stockpot, melt the butter and sauté the onions until they begin to turn golden.

Add the flour and stir it in. Add the chicken stock, wine and *bouquet garni* and continue to simmer on low heat for at least 40 minutes.

Slice the baguette into small slices and broil one side until just toasted. After the soup has simmered, remove the *bouquet garni* and add the soup to ovenproof bowls and place a slice of bread in the middle of each one.

Cover each bowl with cheese and place them on a cookie sheet for easy handling. Place the tray of soup under a medium high broiler flame until the cheese reaches your desired doneness.

Slaw Salad

-salade de choux cru

You will need:
1 head of purple cabbage
1 head of green cabbage
1 cup of mayonnaise (see page 46)
½ cup of sugar
¼ cup of red wine vinegar
Plenty of sea salt and pepper

Shred cabbage with your food processor or chop into desired size with a sharp knife. In a separate bowl combine the mayonnaise, sugar and red wine vinegar until the sugar is dissolved. Combine everything thoroughly.

Salt and pepper to taste.

Serve cold. Any leftovers can be stored in the fridge for a few days.

Cole slaw, the taste of summer. By making the dressing you can serve it to your family with confidence that there is no high fructose corn syrup and that you are giving them the best of the best. Serve with hamburgers and a side of swimming in the pool!

This recipe makes enough to take to a big summer cookout or to have left overs in the fridge all weekend long.

Summer Broccoli Salad

-salade fraîche de broccoli

You will need:
4 bunches of broccoli
1 cup of onion
1 cup of raisins (tri-color raisins add beauty)
2 cups of crumbled, crispy bacon
4 cups of mayonnaise (see page 46)
1 cup of evaporated cane juice
8 tablespoons red wine vinegar

Wash and chop broccoli into small pieces. Chop the onion until it begins to release its juice. Combine broccoli, onion and raisins in the serving bowl. In a separate bowl mix together the mayonnaise, evaporated cane juice and red wine vinegar. Pour mayonnaise mixture over the broccoli and at crumbled bacon. Serves 8.

This is a staple at our family cookouts and I always harass my Gramma that she didn't make enough. Oh! The variety of tastes and textures. Come on, I don't mean to over analyze a simple salad but the is one of my favorites but I could literally eat the entire thing myself. In fact, once when I was pregnant... I did. Homemade mayonnaise and onion juice gives it extra character and set it apart from traditional cole slaw.

Blue Cheese and Bean Potato Salad

-salade de pommes de terre au fromage bleu

Start by boiling water. Cut your potatoes in halves or quarters, depending on how big they are, and cook them in the boiling water until they are medium soft. Do not cook them beyond a medium soft stage or else they will become mealy when assembling the salad. Strain and place them in a serving bowl and very lightly mash one third of the potatoes with a fork to crumble them a bit.

Fry the bacon and set aside. Pour the remaining bacon grease in a bowl and set aside. Steam the green beans to the point of them being crisp cooked. Strain and allow them to cool slightly before adding them to the potatoes. Lightly drizzle the green beans with a couple tablespoons of the bacon grease. Gently mix the potatoes, green beans, bacon and a couple spoonfuls of the bacon grease. Add blue cheese crumbles according to taste and toss the salad with balsamic vinaigrette. Salt and pepper to taste.

Let the salad rest a few hours before serving for serving.

You will need:
Potatoes (tri-color)
Green beans
Bacon
Balsamic vinaigrette (see page 33)
Blue cheese crumbles
Sea salt to taste
Freshly ground flower pepper (see page 41)

Choose your quantities based on how much salad you'd like to make. You can't ruin this twist on potato salad because the flavors are so delicious together. I use equal parts potatoes and green beans.

Farm Style Green Beans
-haricots verts à la paysanne

Many of my most vivid memories take place at my Grandparent's farm outside Remington, Indiana. Once a map-dot of a town, it's now surrounded by turbines and Big Ag. I loved being there so much as a child. So much so in fact I am sure I am the only one aware of the impact that the farm and its inhabitants have had on my life. With growth in the area some things are a little different now but the warm company, stories told and food remain the same.

I have countless, countless memories of swimming all day in the pool and coming up out of the water to hear the gravel crunch as a pickup rolled down the driveway. Moments later the sound of bare feet running and a holler shouted into the air, my Grampa would jump into the pool in his cut-off jeans, scorched from a long day in the field. Oh! How we would squeal when Grandpa would join us. No sooner would he get cooled off then Gram would call us in for "supper."

Dinner during our visits would almost always consist of grilled hamburgers, deviled eggs, potato chips, homemade chip dip, broccoli salad, green beans and slices of cantaloupe. The memories are so clear I can almost feel my wet bathing suit clinging to my skin and sense the boredom of waiting for our food to digest so we could swim into the darkness, just the Junebugs and us.

Gram is eighty-three today and if you visit the farm today you're likely to be fed the same fair just as lovingly made as it was thirty years ago. Though the pool is gone and so are Grampa's farming and pool jumping days, you can still enjoy listening to his stories of years gone by and of his hope for an eternity with his Savior Jesus.

You will need:
One pound of fresh or frozen green beans
Half pound of bacon
Two tablespoons of butter
One small onion or three young onions

Fry the bacon in a skillet and slice onions into thin rings. Do not discard the bacon grease. Allow the bacon to cool after frying and crumble it into small pieces and set aside.

In a medium saucepan add one inch of water and your green beans and steam until they are crisp. Do not over cook. Strain remaining water and add the butter, mixing thoroughly.

Add crumbled bacon and onions to the green beans and drizzle one or two tablespoons of the bacon grease over the top.

Apples and Onions

-pommes et oignons

In a day and age that is lacking in true heroes on our family has found a true admiration in Laura Ingalls Wilder and her husband Almanzo. Farmer Boy, the book Laura wrote about her husband's beautiful childhood is a cult classic in our home. The passages and their descriptions about a little boy craving his mother's cooking bring a smile to my face and inspire me to dote on my boys.

Apples and Onions is mentioned more than once in the book and one autumn day when apples were hanging heavy from our neighbors trees the children and I decided to give it a try based on the description in the book. Of course, we added flavors that Mother Wilder probably did not use like balsamic vinegar and thyme.

I highly recommend this as an accompaniment to your favorite steak, chicken or with your Thanksgiving turkey. My children will eat a large bowl of apples and onions and consider it a complete meal.

You will need:
8 baking apples (McIntosh or Empire), sliced ½ inch to ¼ inch thickness
5 yellow onions
5 tablespoons of butter
Fresh thyme
Balsamic vinegar to taste
Salt and pepper to taste

Slice onions into thin rings by hand or with a food processor.

In a large skillet melt the butter and add the onions. Cook until the begin to turn golden. Add the apples and continue to sauté, moving the mixture around with a wooden spoon.

When the apples and onions are golden and soft sprinkle with the fresh thyme and drizzle with balsamic vinegar if you desire. These are absolutely fabulous with pork or your Thanksgiving turkey.

Serves 4–6 depending on if your children love it like mine do!

Parisienne Farmgirl hint:
Variations on a theme... Want to modernize Mother Wilder's recipe even more? Try adding sautéed beets and roasted pine nuts to the mixture. Fold in Mascarpone cheese too!

Peas -n- Cream

-petit pois à la crème

Starchy, tiny and sweet, peas are my favorite. I'm content to eat a big bowl of steamed peas with a large pat of butter and the crunch of sea salt. On our farm we grow the 1840's heirloom, Champion of England. The children love to set the sturdy seeds, tucking them safely in the ground. They wait with anticipation as the coiling seedling pushing it's way out of the soil is a sure sign that spring is fully underway.

While a bowl of peas can hold it's own in my book, when I'm looking for even more flavor I'll take them for a spin this way. Peas, béchamel, caramelized onions... need I say more?

You will need:
One pound of fresh or frozen peas
Water for steaming
Béchamel sauce (see page 42)
2 onions, minced and caramelized
¼ cup of crème fraîche (see page 115)
Sea salt, cracked pepper and freshly ground nutmeg to taste

Mince the onions, but not so much that they become watery. In a small skillet caramelize them until they begin to golden. Remove them from the skillet and set aside and proceed to make the Béchamel sauce (page 42).

In a medium saucepan steam the peas until just done. Strain the remaining water and add the Béchamel sauce and onions. Gently fold in the crème fraîche and serve promptly.

Serves 4 and can be doubled.

Potager Pizza
-pizza de potagère

There are no exact measurements for this recipe. It's all about a stroll through your summer potager and gathering what's available. The combination of vegetables I have included here simply happen to be my favorite.

If you're pressed for time and don't want to make homemade pizza, don't fret Momma. Some days are simply about surviving. Break out your favorite frozen pizza and add bake according to the directions with these vegetables slathered all over the top. I promise, I won't tell anyone.

You will need:
Pizza dough (see recipe page 173)
Pasta sauce (see recipe page 44)
Broccoli
Leeks
Yellow onion
Beets
Butter
Fresh herbs

In a large skillet melt the butter (extra butter will make your vegetables even better). Add everything but the broccoli and sauté until they start to become soft and some of the onions begin to turn golden. Add the broccoli and continue to sauté until it is heated through and slightly cooked. Sautéing broccoli releases its fabulous nutty flavor! Spread across your uncooked pizza and bake at 425 until the cheese is your desired color. We like ours golden brown and well done.

*Eat leeks in March and wild garlic in May
And all year after physicians may play.*

Old Welsh Rhyme

Braised Leeks

-poireaux braisés

Leeks. An addiction.

Nothing, absolutely nothing says "potager" or French kitchen garden like a sturdy row of leeks. *À mon avis*, In my opinion they are the quintessential French garden vegetable. I love the firmness with which they grow, like little soldiers in a row and the flavor this "gourmet onion" bring to soups, egg dishes and pot pies is unparalleled.

You will need 6–8 small leeks or 4 large
2 tablespoons of extra virgin olive oil
½ cup of chicken stock
¼ cup – ½ cup of grated Romano
Sea salt and pepper to taste

Remove the greens. Cut the leeks down the center and open them up, thoroughly rinsing them under cold water. Pat dry. In a large skillet fry the leeks on the open side for five minutes and on the back side for 3 minutes. Add the stock and sprinkle with salt, pepper and Romano cheese and bake at 375 for 8–10 minutes or until the stock has evaporated.

Herbed Farm Potatoes, Two Ways

-pommes de terre aux herbes façon paysanne

Potatoes are a staple on our farm. Yellow potatoes, purple potatoes and red ones too. Each spring the planting of potatoes signifies the beginning are the gardening season in our zone and the entire family pitches in to help dig the trenches, spread the compost and plant the potatoes, using a twelve inch stick to make sure they are evening spaced! I wish I could say everyone is equally as excited to help *hill* the potatoes throughout the season, but by the time harvest time comes around everyone is excited to help again. We all get giddy when the pitchfork props up a handful of potatoes with a plunge into the ground. Downright giddy.

I store our potatoes in the pantry, unwashed, in between layers of paper in wine crates. We enjoy them all winter long.

Herbes de Provence and garlic offer potatoes a chance to really shine and of course a little fat; either olive oil or butter.

For Herbed Farm Potato French Fries you will need:
Yukon Gold Potatoes sliced into ½ inch wedges
Olive oil
Garlic, minced
Herbes de Provence
Sea salt
Cracked pepper

All ingredients are to taste.

Preheat the oven to 425 degrees.

Shake all the ingredients together in a sealed plastic bag and bake at 425 until they reach your desired doneness. We like everything really well done around here! And we love to eat these with steak and homemade mayonnaise (see page 46).

For Herbed Breakfast Potatoes you will need:
Yukon Gold Potatoes sliced into 1 inch to ½ inch cubes
Olive oil, butter or goose fat
Garlic, minced
Scallions
Herbes de Provence
Sea salt
Cracked pepper

All ingredients are to taste. Mix everything together in a large bowl. Heat your fat of choice in a large cast iron skillet and fry until the potatoes reach your desired doneness.

Serve with over easy eggs or Sugared Eggs on page 138.

Cauliflower Gratin

-chou-fleur au gratin

You will need:
2 pounds of cauliflower
8 ounces of salted butter
½ cup of flour
3 cups of whole milk
3 bay leaves
Grated nutmeg to taste
2 tablespoons white wine mustard
4 cups grated Swiss or Emmental cheese, divided
Salt and pepper to taste

A delicious classic French dish quickly becomes a farm staple. Perfect for that strange, cool day in July or the middle of winter when savory, flavor filled vegetables fit the bill.

I make this dish to serve a good 6–8 people because it's so delicious.

You will see the roots of this sauce lie in Béchamel sauce the vegetable is accommodated by adding bay leaf and cheese.

Begin by blanching the cauliflower until it begins to become tender in lightly salted water and set aside.

In a separate, heavy-duty saucepan melt the butter and add the flour, mixing thoroughly. Add the milk and bay leaf. Season with nutmeg and allow the mixture to simmer for five minutes.

After five minutes remove the pan from the heat and remove the bay leaf. Add the two cups of the cheese and mustard stir until melted.

Add the blanched cauliflower to an oven-proof dish and pour the sauce over top sprinkling with the remaining cheese. Bake for 15–25 minutes until browned and bubbling.

From France to the Farm • 83

Sweet Carrots

-carottes douces

There is almost always a sequence to my cooking. I spend many hours a day in the kitchen and so I do what I call "cooking down." I start with one thing like a roast chicken, which leads to stock, which leads to risotto, which leads to leftovers for lunch the next day. A day of baking bread leads to grilled cheese sandwiches for lunch, French toast the next day and then stale bread crumbs for the chickens.

I grew up on these Sweet Carrots paired with a Sunday Pot Roast and then used in the tomato vegetable soup. Cooking down.

You will need:
2 pounds of carrots
2 cups of water
4 tablespoons butter
1 tablespoon of fresh thyme plus an additional sprig for garnish
¼ cup brown sugar (page 35)

Cut and wash carrots. In a medium saucepan with a lid steam over medium-high heat for 15–20 minutes. Strain most of the water and add butter, brown sugar and thyme. Garnish with a sprig of thyme.

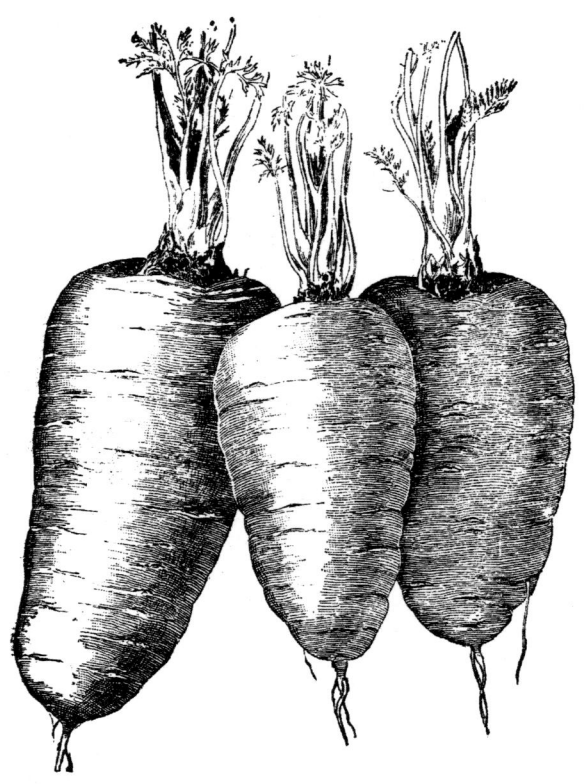

Meats

Pot Roast

-boeuf à la mode

My Great Gramma's family heritage comes from the Alsace, Lorraine area. This is the area of eastern France that, over the years has switched back and forth from France to Germany and back again. So much so that all my great grandparents spoke German. A legacy I wish had been handed down to all of us. I hope to one day visit the family town of Strasbourg, France.

It should come as no surprise that something as delicious as the pot roast has it's roots found in France! I bet my Gramma doesn't even know this, but boy, can she make a pot roast! She taught my mom, and sure enough, one day I called my mom... "Mom, how do you make a pot roast?"

What I love about our family recipes is that there is a consistency throughout each kitchen, yet every woman has her own take on the family classics. This is my take on this family classic and dare I say, *c'est incroyable!* It would be shameful for me to be too proud, lest I step on much respected toes!

Serves 6-8 with a little left over for soup.

Rolled Sirloin Tip (sometimes referred to as a rolled rump roast, with strings)
(If you use a Chuck Roast it's very fatty and you will get a different taste)
2-3 cups of kosher salt, divided
2 Bay leaves
1 head of garlic, separated
3-4 medium onions, sliced thin
2 cups of dry red wine
Kitchen Bouquet sauce to taste, a couple tablespoons may do (page 43)
Fresh herbs (Rosemary, sage and thyme)
Water (amount depends on the roasting pan size but it should be one inch deep)
Carrots, cut into two inch pieces
New potatoes, quartered

Preheat oven to 425 degrees.

Fill a large pot with cold water and add 1 cup of the kosher salt. Mix well. Add the meat and allow it to soak in the kosher water for thirty minutes. Rinse the meat and discard the water. Cover the meat in the remaining kosher salt and allow it to rest for another thirty minutes and then rinse and pat dry. Sprinkle onion powder, pepper and salt over the meat. Begin by quickly searing the meat on all sides in a heavy duty, hot skillet. Upon searing, remove from heat.

Fill a roasting pan with one inch of water and add the bay leaves, sliced onions, sprigs of rosemary and sage, garlic and dry red wine. Add the meat and cook uncovered at 425 degrees until the top begins to look crusty. Once it begins to look crusty add the carrots, quartered potatoes any other vegetables of choice, like mushrooms. Cover with the roaster lid and turn it down to 300 degrees and cook approximately two hours for a three-pound roast.
If you're roast is bigger or smaller simply check it's doneness occasionally by slicing a small opening in the center of the meat and taking a peak. If you prefer a very well done roast, simply wait until the strings fall apart during the cooking as a sign of its doneness. We prefer ours a bit more rare.

Garnish with fresh herbs. Remember, a little green on any plate adds always adds loveliness!

For the gravy:
3 tablespoon unsalted butter
2 tablespoon of flour
Juices left in the roasting pan, about 2 cups

To make the gravy use a slotted spoon and transfer the meat and vegetables to a serving platter. Remove the bay leaves and any fats on the top of the cooking liquids. You can strain the liquid and bring it to a new saucepan if you'd prefer. (It will be about two cups.) Heat on medium low and add the butter. Once it has melted, add the flour and whisk until blended. Bring the mixture to a simmer and whisk until thickened and reduced to the thickness you desire. Freeze any leftover gravy for Shepherd's Pie.

Salt Crust Chicken with Rosemary

-poulet de croûte de sel au romarin

This is a classic French technique for preparing a chicken, and if you are looking for a new way to make America's favorite bird, may I suggest this favorite method of my husbands. Now, don't get me wrong. HE is not preparing the dish but this is the method that he prefers I use. He's right. It's very easy, tastes incredible and is a pleasant change from the more popular roast chicken.

You will need:
1 roaster chicken
1 box of kosher salt
Fresh rosemary sprigs

Equipment:
Dutch oven
Tack hammer or something to break the baked salt crust

Preheat the oven to 475 degrees.

Pour two cups of salt in the bottom of the Dutch oven. Place the rosemary sprigs on top of the salt. Rinse the chicken in cold water and pat dry. Place the chicken on top of rosemary. Place additional sprigs around and on top of the chicken. Pour salt all around and on top of the chicken completely covering it. It should be covered by at least one inch of salt on top. Cover the dish and bake for 1 ½ hours.

Carefully use a small tack hammer to break open the salt crust. You can set it aside, let it cool and save it for the next time if you want. You will not want to save the rosemary, as it will be well cooked.

From France to the Farm

Pork Loin with Herbs and Scallions

-échine de porc aux herbes et aux oignons blancs

This one happened by accident, and what a happy accident it was! I was pressed for time and the only meat I had thawed was a pork loin however, roasting it in the oven for an hour was not an option. We had a little league game to attend! I made a mad dash out to the herb garden, grabbed what I could and started chopping herbs and slicing little medallions of pork. What began as an effort to get a little boy to a ball game with a full stomach has become a family favorite.

This recipe is a great example of what you can create when you grow herbs and keep basics on hand like cream and lots of butter!

You will need:
1 large handful of your favorite herbs
1 stick of salted butter, softened, divided
1 medium sized pork loin
3–5 green onions
2 cups of heavy cream

Pat the pork loin dry with a cloth napkin or paper towel and slice into medallions about one inch thick. Finely chop the herbs and mix them with half of the butter. Chop the green onions and set aside. Salt and pepper the pork medallions and spread the butter mixture onto the top of each one.

In a heavy skillet on low/medium heat melt the remaining butter. Fry the medallions in the pan herb/butter side up, 2–4 minutes per side and then transfer to a plate.

Turn the heat down and scrape up any bits on the bottom of the pan with a wooden spoon. Add cream and increase the heat, stirring until the sauce darkens a bit and reduces by about a third. Strain with a fine sieve and pour into a gravy bowl.

Place the meat on a serving plate or individual plates; pour the sauce over the top and sprinkle with fresh green onions.

This meat is excellent when served with a crusty loaf of bread and green beans. A Beaujolais is nice with a pork loin.

Half-Way Hamburgers
-hamburgers façon ferme à mi-chemin

On Half-Way Farm we love to entertain around our fire-pit. Sometimes you have to set frou-frou food aside and have a good old American cookout! I make these burgers up the night before so I can relax with my cookout company as much as possible. They are a great excuse to use the herbs and green onions that are so bountiful in the spring and summer gardens. This makes about seven hamburgers and of course can be duplicated or reduced.

I insist you serve them with the homemade buns! The ones in this cookbook of course.

You will need:
2 pounds of ground beef
1 handful of herbs (parsley, sage, chives)
2 green table onions chopped thin
1 large egg
1 cup of feta cheese (optional)
Dash of sea salt
Dash of pepper

Combine, shape into patties and grill!

Garden Tacos
-tacos aux legumes du jardin

For the meat you will need:

Two pound grass-fed ground beef or one boiled broiler chicken, meat removed and shredded in the food processor.
½ cup of water
2 ½ tablespoons of cumin
1 tablespoon of cayenne (omit for a milder taster)
1 teaspoon of chili powder
½ teaspoon of paprika
½ teaspoon of sugar
½ teaspoon of garlic salt
Adjust seasonings according to taste.

I could eat tacos every day of the week. In our house every night could be taco night and no one would complain. We like our tacos pretty authentic, so I make my own seasoning for the ground beef and in season we raid the garden for colorful vegetables. Add what you'd like but these are simple, delicious, Mexican tacos.

In a large skillet add the water and meat and fry the meat on medium to high heat until it is half done. Add the spices and continue to cook until meat is finished cooking.

Assemble and garnish with:
1 package of small soft, corn tortillas
1 round of queso fresco
1 sliced red onion if desired
Loose leaves of red heirloom lettuce
Salsa (Diced tomato, onion, jalapeño, cilantro and salt pulsed in a food processor)

Shepherd's Pie

-hachis Parmentier

Shepherd's Pie. The very name says comfort food. I think nowadays the term comfort food has a bad rap, but what is food if not to nourish us and comfort us? Food comforts our stressed bodies and souls with an opportunity to sit down and use our five senses while enjoying one another's company.

Shepherd's Pie does just that, with creamy mashed potatoes, sweet, caramelized onions, firm corn and hearty beef. This meal brings a smile to my husband's face if he sees it on the counter ready to be served after a long day of work. We also serve it as our unconventional Resurrection Sunday meal with a lamb cake for dessert.

Preparation of this meal requires all four or six burners of your range. All the ingredients can be prepared a day or two ahead and refrigerated, however, I do not recommend making the carrots in advance.

Serves 6–8.

For the potatoes layer you will need:
3 pounds of potatoes
1 cup of sour cream or crème fraîche
4 tablespoons of butter

For the beef layer:
2 pounds of ground beef
¼ cup of water

For the onion layer:
5 yellow or sweet onions
5–8 tablespoons butter

For the corn layer:
4 cups of corn

For the carrot layer:
4 cups of baby carrots
2 tablespoons of butter
¼ cup of brown sugar (See page 35)

The potatoes:
Bring a stockpot of water to a full boil. While the water is boiling peel your potatoes and quarter. Cook the potatoes until they are soft and blend with a hand held blender until chunky. Add the butter and sour cream or crème fraîche. Resume blending until smooth. Salt.

The ground beef:
While the potatoes are cooking, fry the ground beef in a large skillet. Add a small amount of water and chop the meat up with a square wooden spoon as it cooks. Adding a little water will keep it from getting dry. Once cooked, remove with a slotted spoon. If preparing the same day begin to layer your pie by laying the ground beef on the bottom of a casserole dish. Pour some of the remaining meat juices over the top and continue layering as your other items are ready.

For the onions:
Peel and slice onions into thin rings by hand or with the slicing attachment of your food processor. In another skillet melt the butter and sauté the onions until caramelized. Spread them on top of the meat layer in the casserole when finished.

For the carrots:
Follow the Sweet Carrots recipe on page 87 and add to the existing layers.

For the corn:
Simply steam the corn in a small saucepan, strain and add it to your pie layers.

The potato topper:
Spread your mashed potatoes across the top of your pie and bake at 375 degrees until they begin to golden.

For the gravy use your wonderful gravy you froze from your pot roast leftovers!

I am the Good Shepherd. The Good Shepherd lays down his life for his friends.
John 10:11

Parisienne Pot Pie
-tarte à la Parisienne

It was late in the afternoon and I thought to myself, "I should try to make a chicken pot pie. How hard can it be?" Then I remembered all the leeks I had stored in the freezer and my love for Béchamel sauce and the inspiration overtook me to create the loveliest chicken potpie ever.

Like, ever!

I played around a bit with my tart crust, added flower pepper, fresh calendula and rosemary leaves and did I mention, *a lot* of butter? I hated putting this one in the oven. The dough was simply so pretty.

Of course, you can make this dough without the edible flowers... but why would you?

This is a beautiful way to capture the edible blooms in your garden as it can be frozen and enjoyed one cold winter evening.

Serves 8.

For the filling you will need:
The meat from one boiled chicken or meat leftover from yesterdays roast chicken, shredded
8 tablespoons of butter
4 cups of leeks, sliced thin
1 onion, minced
2 cups of peas, fresh or frozen
1 cup of carrots, fresh or frozen, thin sliced

For the crust, follow the Shortcrust recipe on page 164, doubled.

For the sauce, follow the Béchamel sauce recipe on page 42, doubled.

Begin by boiling your chicken for one hour (if you don't have chicken leftovers) and by making the dough. Before chilling it as mentioned in that recipe split your dough ball in two.

After it has chilled and you begin to roll it out take your favorite herbs and edible flowers and gently lay them on top of one of the pieces (you only need to decorate the top crust). Carefully continue to roll out the dough until you have the shape of the top of your pie. Make it slightly larger than the dish you are using, so you have extra dough for pinching the top dough and bottom dough together.

Roll out the bottom dough and press it into your dish making sure the dough hangs up and over the edges slightly. In a large skilled, melt the butter and sauté your vegetables while you begin to make your Béchamel sauce. Sauté them enough so they are coated in the butter and cooked slightly. When your sauce is made and your vegetables are sautéed add your Béchamel sauce, chicken and vegetables into your prepared dish. It if piles high that is O.K.

Take the lovely top crust and drape it over the top and working around the edges pinch the two crusts together to seal everything in.

Bake on 375 until the crust is golden brown. If your pie was very full you may want to put a cookie sheet on the rack below to catch any overflow.

Parisienne Farmgirl hint:
When your edible flowers are in full bloom, make up a handful of potpie top crusts and freeze them so you can enjoy their beauty on your Parisienne Pot Pie's all winter.

Wait 'til you see those baked Nasturtium petals.
They look like fragile tissue paper!

Perfectly Roasted Chicken
-poulet roti à la perfection

Here on Half-Way Farm chickens are a family operation. We order chicks from the hatchery every spring and raise them for about three months. We pasture them and supplement them with organic feed. Sometimes we butcher them ourselves, and sometimes we have it done for us and then we fill our freezer with chicken for the year. This provides us with plenty of meals and a variety of meat as we trade with other homesteaders for salmon and venison. We eat one roast chicken a week and then I make chicken stock for the freezer or subsequent meals.

No store bought chicken can compare with a pastured, farm-raised chicken. Pastured chickens graze on bugs and grass all day long providing them with plenty of nutrients and Omega 3's. You can find this healthy meat by word of mouth in rural areas and on Craigslist. Quality farmers will be happy to show you around and show you where your dinner is coming from. And if you have the space and are truly adventurous why not try raising your own? We select chicks that come from stock completely free of genetically modified feed.

You will need:
One, fresh or previously frozen free-range chicken
15–20 cloves of garlic (more to taste if you love garlic like we do)
Herbes de Provence (thyme, bay leaf, rosemary and oregano)
1 slice of slightly stale bread
Olive oil
1 bunch of fresh carrots
2 yellow or sweet onions
Sea salt, pepper and paprika to taste

Generously drizzle olive oil or spread butter on the skin of the chicken. Sprinkle with salt, pepper, paprika and Herbes de Provence. Rub the bread with one of the garlic cloves and stuff it into the cavity. Add a couple cloves of garlic to the cavity. Clean the carrots and slice them into 3–4 inch long sections. Peel and quarter the onions.

Add the chicken to a medium large roasting pan and scatter the carrots, garlic and potatoes around the sides.

Bake at 375 for one hour and until juice from thigh is clear when pricked.

Smoked Salmon Crêpes with Crème Fraîche

-crêpes de saumon fumé à la crème fraîche

At the corner of the Boulevard Saint Michel and the Quai Saint Michel is the Depot Saint Michel. It's nothing fancy but it makes for *phenomenal* people watching when weary feet need a rest from walking the streets of Paris.

I ordered this plate once after a long day of exploring, and it became a favorite upon recreating it at home.

There are few measurements for this recipe as you are free to fill your *crêpes* as thin or as thick as you'd like them. Add a touch of lemon juice *et voilà*... just like the Depot Saint Michel, minus the people watching of course. For that, you'll have to use your imagination or buy a plane ticket.

You will need:
Fresh crêpes (see recipe on page 172)
Crème Fraîche (store bought or follow the recipe on page 115)
Smoked salmon pieces
Sliced red onion
Lemon wedge for juicing
Sea salt and pepper to taste

Spread the desired amount of crème fraîche on an open crêpe and layer with the smoked salmon and onion slices. Fold as desired and squirt with fresh lemon juice. Remember, the warmer the crêpe the faster your crème fraîche will melt. If they are freshly made you may want to allow them to cool a bit.

If you are making many for a family meal layer your crêpes with parchment paper in a stack as you cook them.

From France to the Farm • 103

Chicken and Noodles

-poulet et nouilles

Few tastes conjure up my childhood like Chicken and Noodles. Gramma used to make them all the time and in our family we eat them with thick, homemade applesauce on the side. Rich, hearty and totally satisfying, this meal is an easy fix when you have noodles made up and you've been making chicken stock that day. If you're in a pinch, wide, store-bought egg noodles will do. Don't play the martyr. Just feed the people, woman!

You will need:
Homemade pasta (see page 180)
Shredded chicken (like the kind you can peal right off the carcass while your stock is cooking)
½–1 cup of chicken stock
8 ounces of butter
2–4 tablespoons of flour

Adjust ratios for your serving size. One batch of homemade pasta serves four.

If you are making your own pasta you can try hand cutting your noodles for an extra wide option. Cook your pasta to desired texture. We prefer *al dente* for this dish. Nothing like a big, thick, chewy noodle! In a small saucepan add the butter to the hot chicken stock. Mix in the flour by whisking briskly and pour over cooked pasta. Shred chicken and mix it all together. Salt and pepper to taste. Extra pepper is wonderful!

Grandpa & Gramma's Farm Circa 1950

Summer Steak with Herb Butter
-bifteck au beurre persillé

Steak with herbed butter is quintessential bistro food and here on the farm it's a go-to meal since we are always looking for ways to use the abundance of herbs we grow each summer and we're always looking for an excuse to build a fire. For the perfect Parisienne Farmgirl meal serve this with the Herbed Potatoes and Homemade Mayonnaise and you've got the best of both worlds; a French classic with elements of the homegrown that will melt in your mouth. Don't forget a big, bad red for your glass of wine. Of course, this can be made indoors on the stove top too, in your favorite cast iron skillet.

You will need:
Quality free range steaks, preferably filet mignon or flank steak, 1 inch thick.
Clarified butter (two tablespoons per steak)
Herbed butter (see page 158) add minced shallots if desired, two to four tablespoons of butter per steak
Sea salt and pepper to taste

Season your steaks with salt and pepper on both sides. On medium heat or over a hot, established fire, melt the butter in a large stainless steel or cast iron skillet. Do not let it brown. Clarified butter burns faster than regular butter. (If cooking over a fire simply raise and lower your tripod to raise and lower the heat over which you are cooking) Increase heat to high and sear steaks on both sides. Reduce the heat to medium and cook, turning occasionally until desired doneness. About ten minutes for an excellent *à point* or medium rare steak.

Serve with sautéed broccoli, onions and mushrooms.

Parisienne Farmgirl hint:
When ordering steak at any French restaurant use the following expressions:
Saignant for rare
Bien cuit for well done
But for a perfectly prepared steak at any French restaurant order it *à point*... medium rare perfection!

On Copper

It was a dreary day in Paris. My heart pounded in my chest as the metro bumped along towards the flea market. *Vanves*. What would I find? Would I be able to afford anything? Would I be able to lug it back to my apartment by myself? It had been two years since my last visit and I hadn't stopped thinking about it since.

   Everything was as I remembered. The lady with the wonderful textiles was there. Wall-to-wall people and affordable treasures were everywhere I turned.

I found myself gently shoving my way to the front of many stalls to rummage through boxes that were strewn along the ground and there I spotted it; a huge, thick, heavy copper pot. It was marked 90 Euros. Only slightly out of my budget but I had only just begun, and I didn't want to use such a large chunk of my spending money within my first thirty minutes.

   In my very best French I tried to bargain with the vendeur. I low-balled him with a 60 Euro offer. *Oh, no, no, mademoiselle!* I tried again, *Alors, je n'ai pas quatre-vingt dix euros. C'est trop cher.* He tried to woo me with his copper pot. He knew I wanted it badly. Back and forth we went but I shrugged and offered him a very French, *Merci, non* and walked away.

I shopped. Plates, pillowcases, an ancient watercolor set but still the copper called to me.

   The lunch hour was coming and the market was winding down. If it was still there, now would be my chance. We locked eyes as I walked up and he knew what I wanted, *Soixante euros?* I asked again, batting my lashes. *Oui mademoiselle.* He sighed in defeat. *Soixante euros.*

   As I lugged that copper pot home in the rain, I felt as high as a kite. It was my very first piece of copper and every time I see it on my kitchen wall I remember the drizzly day at the marché de Vanves when I went ten rounds for what I wanted... and won.

Copper is a favorite of professionals and amateurs alike because of its superior heat conductivity. Copper is perfect for choice cuts of meat that require special attention to temperature. A copper pan heats uniformly, reducing the risk of overcooking the meat in the center of the pan and undercooking the cuts placed on the outer edges of the pan. Precise heat is easy to reach with copper cookware as it responds immediately to changes in heat. Copper will do the work for you. Never mind that it is absolutely beautiful and evokes a French farmhouse sort of feeling in any kitchen. It is without a doubt the iconic kitchen cookware, which is why many cooks chose to display their copper as opposed to hiding it away in the cupboards. Copper pots hung on the walls say, "I mean business. Have a seat. Dinner is on the way."

Cleaning copper is worth the effort. As a soft metal, copper is the best heat conducting metal available for your kitchen. Cleaning your copper will actually protect the heat conductivity as areas of tarnish can suffer. Your supermarket carries copper cleaners and no doubt you have items in your pantry that will do the trick too, even tomato paste can be used. Cover the pot and let it sit for a few minutes and then simply wash it off. This is my method of choice for lightly tarnished copper. You can cut a lemon in two, cover the lemon with salt and scrub your pot, then polish it with a soft cloth. You can also use baking soda and lemon juice. For heavy duty grime and patina I swear by Mauviels's "Copperbrill." For spotless copper you want to clean your pots and pans after every use however, if you appreciate a certain patina then you will only clean your pots occasionally.

Stores like Sur la Table and Williams Sonoma carry absolutely beautiful copper that will make you feel like a pro just by placing it on your stove and it's easy to find fun pieces of copper with which to decorate your kitchen. It's a bit more difficult to find quality copper second hand though and when you do it's likely to need a little TLC.

If your copper pots are scratched on the interior and the tin has been scraped away to reveal the copper below, for safety, you will want to have your piece re-tinned. There are only a couple of companies in America who re-tin copper. I suggest East Coast Tinning. (www.eastcoasttinning.com) If you found your copper for a steal this is a very worthy investment. You can even have your monogram engraved in the side making a copper pot into a true family heirloom.

The real things haven't changed. It is still best to be honest and truthful; to make the most of what we have; to be happy with simple pleasures; and have courage when things go wrong.

Laura Ingalls Wilder

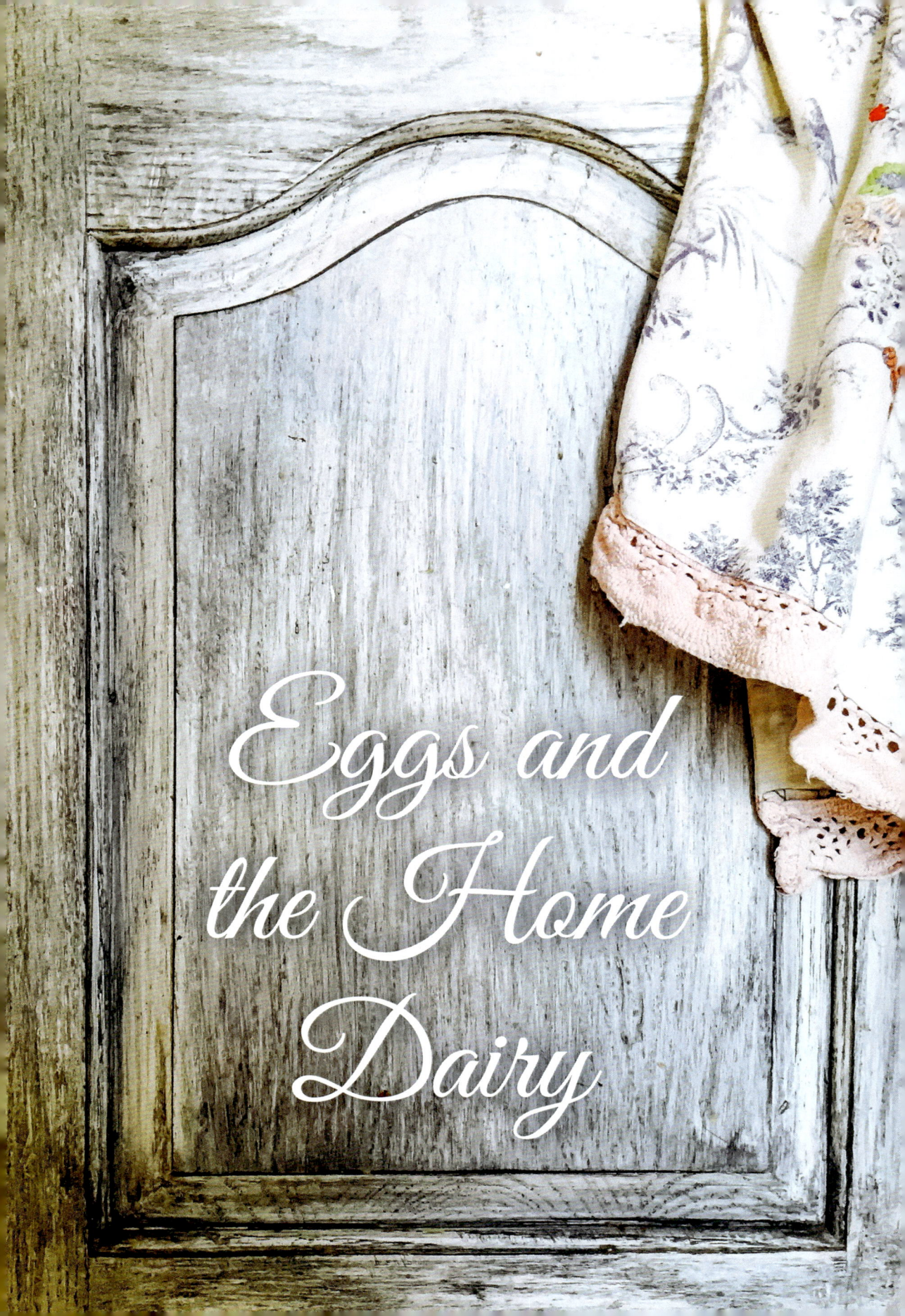

Greek Yogurt

-yaourt grec

Traditionally Greek yogurt is made from ewe or cow's milk and so I make ours each week with cow's milk from a local farmer. If you don't have a raw milk source you can make yours with store bought milk, though I do suggest using whole milk for the fullest taste. Unlike regular yogurt, Greek yogurt is known for being very thick and I personally find it much more satisfying than its runny counterpart. A big bowl of Greek yogurt with honey or berries is a decadent way to start your day. It can also be used in sauces and in guacamole to make it stretch.

By making your own yogurt you can be sure to always have some in stock for enjoyment. Yogurt is not only delicious but also full of live cultures that are great for your digestive tract and the health of you family.

To help with weight management I choose to make a full fat yogurt by using full fat milk. Our farmer raises Jersey cows and one gallon of milk easily has a two to three inch line of cream at the top. I find that eating full fat products gives me the energy that I need to get through the day here on the farm. I also choose not to sweeten my yogurt with vanilla or sugar. If you are used to store bought, pre-sweetened yogurt I suggest switching to plain and allowing your taste buds a week or so to get used to the true taste of yogurt. Once they make the switch you'll fall in love with Greek yogurt and a side of brightly colored berries... if you haven't already.

You will need:
1 gallon of milk
½ cup Greek yogurt heaping (starter)

Special Equipment:
Simple meat thermometer
Stainless steal stockpot

Begin by scalding your milk in your stockpot. This will take about 8 minutes with milk that is cold from the refrigerator. Just as milk begins to bubble, remove from heat, put the lid on and allow it to rest for one hour.

Preheat your oven to 175 degrees. After one hour your milk will be about 110 degrees. Add the Greek yogurt starter and stir it thoroughly with a whisk. After whisking in your yogurt starter turn the oven off. Your oven should have been on just a couple of minutes.

Turn your oven light on and place your stockpot in the oven for 8–10 hours. You will know when it's done if it shifts as a mass when you tilt the pot back and forth from side to side.

Lay your cheesecloth (or thin towel) out over your colander. I use the steamer basket that goes with my stockpot as my colander. Carefully pour the yogurt into the cheesecloth, twist it closed and set the colander back over the pot to catch the whey. Leave it to strain for 8–12 hours depending on the desire thickness. You can refrigerate the whey for future recipes. Store your yogurt in glass jars in the refrigerator for 7–10 days.

Crème Fraîche

Tangy with a bit more bit than sour cream, Crème Fraîche is one of my favorites. I used it in many things from meat dishes to deserts. Store bought, it's cost prohibitive to really use it to all it's capabilities in the kitchen, so making your own opens up an entire new world.

Crème Fraîche is excellent on your favorite meat dishes. Simply mince or purée fresh herbs and shallot and enjoy.

You will need:
2 cups heavy cream
2 tablespoons buttermilk

Combine in a saucepan and heat to no more than 85 degrees. Pour into a sterilized jar and cover with a cloth napkin and allow to rest for 12–24 hours of until thickened. Stir and store in the refrigerator for 24 hours before using. It will keep in the refrigerator for one to two weeks.

When you have about a couple tablespoons left at the bottom of your jar repeat the process all over again substituting the buttermilk for the left over Crème Fraîche.

Coco

Valentino

Feta Cheese
-feta

Feta is a simple cheese for the beginner home diary. For years I was too nervous to make my own cheese, though I wanted to badly. I now understand my foolishness again and I will never pay four dollars for a tiny container of feta again.

We use feta on salads and scrambled eggs almost every day of the week.

You will need:
One gallon of whole cows milk.
Mesophillic Culture
Liquid animal rennet
Sterilized stainless steel pot

In a stainless steel stockpot heat the milk to 86 degrees and then sprinkle one packet or ⅟₁₆ teaspoons of mesophilic culture over the top and stir well. (If you are using store bought milk you will add a ½ teaspoon of calcium chloride mixed into a ¼ cup of water after adding your culture.) Allow your milk to stand for one hour.

Add ½ teaspoon liquid rennet into a ¼ cup of cool water and stir it into your milk allowing it to sit for another hour after stirring.

After an hour has passed cut the curds into one-inch cubes and allow them to rest for five minutes. The curds should cut clean and not shaggy. Check the temperature of the curds. At this point you want them at 86 degrees, so you may need to use a double boiler or gently set the pot into a sink of warm water to maintain that temperature while you stir the curds every five minutes for 15 minutes.

Line a colander with quality cheesecloth and gently pour the curds into the cheesecloth. Gather the edges together and tie so that they can be hung. You may be able to hang them off your kitchen faucet. I have a nail nailed into the inside of a cupboard for just this purpose. Allow the curds to drain for four to six hours. Using a bowl underneath to catch the whey for future use.

After they have drained divide the cheese into a couple sections and sprinkle with salt, turning over to do each side. Allow the cheese to sit out at room temperature for 24 hours, salting two to four times according to taste. The cheese will continue to weep water that you will want to drain off. A total of two to four tablespoons of salt should be used.

Feta can be stored in glass or plastic for up to one week. Get creative and add herbs, seasonings and or olive oil.

Quiche

Real men eat quiche; at least they do on this farm. Brunch aside, eggs, heavy cream, meat and vegetables make quiche a hearty meal.

We love our quiche served with a big salad and a balsamic vinaigrette, a chunk of crusty bread and a glass of red wine. How about you?

For the basic quiche filling you will need:
2 cups of heavy cream
8 eggs
1–2 tablespoons of high quality Dijon mustard
Salt and freshly ground
Herbes de Provence

For the crust follow the Shortcrust recipe on page 164.

Preheat your oven to 400 and use one of the following recipes.

Role out the crust using the recommended method on page 164. Prick multiple holes in the crust and line the inside with aluminum foil draping it out up and over the edges. Fill the inside of the pan with pie beads, dry beans or rice. Bake in a quiche or pie dish at 400 degrees for 10–15 minutes. Remove from the oven and turn the oven down to 350 degrees. Carefully remove the aluminum foil and discard of the beans and rice. If you are using pie beads, allow them to cool before pouring them back in their jar. Using a fork or pastry brush, spread the mustard on the crust and bake for another five minutes before adding the rest of the ingredients. Add the ingredients and bake for about fifty minutes. If you prick the center with a sharp knife it should come out clean. The quiche should be jiggly and custardy.

ZUCCHINI AND CHÈVRE QUICHE
2–3 zucchini
1 small log of chèvre (goat cheese)
Small amount of olive oil

Cut the zucchini into half inch thick slices or thinner if you desire and sauté in olive oil until slightly softened or golden brown. While they are sautéing add Herbes de Provence.

Slice the chèvre into half inch slices and arrange with the zucchini in the crust. Pour egg mixture on top and bake following basic quiche directions.

ONION QUICHE

5 medium sized onions sliced thin
8 tablespoons of butter, divided
Fresh herbs to taste

Sauté onions in the butter until they begin to caramelize.

Spread the onions in the pre-baked quiche crust and pour the egg and cream mixture over the top.

From France to the Farm • 123

Parisienne Farmgirl on Eggs

Ah... eggs.

On Half-Way Farm *la ferme à mi-chemin* we have very happy hens. They cackle and cluck and scratch and peck all over our little three acres with two roosters, Maximus a proud Araucana, and Lord Grantham, a regal French Black Copper Maran with a chest as dignified as though he was cock of Downton Abbey. Don't ask me why I gave my French Black Copper Maran rooster the name of an Englishman, even if he is fiction. I couldn't resist. Our two Black Copper Maran hens are named Lady Grantham and Lady Mary. Trust me, if I ever become a dog person, her name will be Isis.

The rest of our flock consists of Cuckoo Marans, Auracanas with their beautiful blue eggs, White Rocks, Golden and Silverlace Wyandottes, Black Australorps and plenty of reliable Golden Buff's. I am currently babying the most adorable Lavender Orpingtons and preparing to introduce them into the flock.

Though I find it terribly inconvenient (because chickens are messy, messy birds), we let ours pasture on green grass all day long. They reek havoc on any patch of garden they can access but this diet provides us with bright, big golden yolks simply full of omega 3's. In the evenings and winter we supplement them with non-GMO, soy free organic feed and in the summer we fluff the nesting boxes with fragrant herbs from the garden.

I often have a baby in my arms so my daughters gather the eggs for me but a couple times a week, I get to steel out to the coop and gather them myself. I never tire of it. I usually pad over to my herb garden for a handful of herbs covered in morning dew.

To crack a warm egg open for breakfast is a delight, and after all my years of craving and dreaming of farm life, to sprinkle fresh herbs over the top is nothing short of a miracle.

Eggs are indeed "the perfect food" for they bail you out in a pinch, create castle-like peaks while making desserts and provide endless opportunities for culinary creations.

From France to the Farm

Ricotta

You will need:
1 gallon of whole cows milk (Goat's or sheep's milk will work too, I use raw milk but yours does not have to be)
1 teaspoon citric acid mixed into ½ cup cool water
2–5 tablespoons of heavy cream
Sea salt to taste

Equipment:
Large, stainless steel stockpot
Colander
2 large bowls
Quality cheesecloth
Food thermometer

Stir the citric acid/water mixture into your milk. Mixing it well. While stirring, SLOWLY heat your milk to 195–205 degrees. Turn off the heat and leave it completely alone for one hour. After one hour put the bowl in your sink and set a cheesecloth lined colander on top. Pour the curds into the cheesecloth-lined colander and drain for 30–45 minutes depending how dry of a ricotta cheese you want. You can also wrap up the ends of your cheesecloth and hang it to drain. Save the remaining whey in the bowl for your chickens if you have them. Chickens benefit greatly from drinking whey or you can use it to make bread.

Ricotta is excellent with sliced granny smith apples and your favorite dressing for a light salad and can be used in many pasta dishes and of course Apple Ricotta Pancakes.

Mozzarella

Drizzled with olive oil or enhanced with herbs, fresh mozzarella is a real treat and easy for the novice cheese maker.

You will need:
1 gallon of milk, raw or pasteurized
1 ¼ teaspoon of citric acid powder
¼ teaspoon of liquid rennet
½ cup of cool water, divided

Equipment:
Large, stainless steel stockpot
Colander
Food thermometer
Long knife or icing tool to cut the curds
Clean, heavy-duty, new rubber gloves.
Small saucepan

Pour the milk into a stainless steal stockpot. In a measuring cup mix the citric acid in ¼ cup of the cool water and mix it into the milk.

Gently warm the milk to 88 degrees. If your milk is cold, just out of the refrigerator, this can take about 8 to 12 minutes on low/medium heat.

In a measuring cup mix a ¼ teaspoon of rennet into a ¼ cup of cool water. Once your milk has reached 88 degrees gently move it to a different (cool) burner so it does not continue to heat and add the water and rennet mixture. Mix thoroughly for ten to fifteen seconds. Allow the milk to rest for fifteen minutes as it turns into curds.

The curds should now make a clean break when you cut into them. Cut them into one-inch cubes by running the knife in lines in one direction the width of the pot and then the other. It should look like a checkerboard. Allow the curds to rest for ten minutes or so.

While the curds are resting, secure the drain on your sink so it does not leak and fill the sink half way full with extremely hot water. After the curds have rested carefully place the stockpot down into the water, taking care that none spills into the pot. The curds should slowly reheat to 108 degrees. They need to stay this temperature for 35 minutes so you may need to add hot or boiling water during this time. Stir them every couple of minutes so the curds don't form back together. After 35 minutes drain the curds into a colander.

In a small saucepan heat some water until it reaches a soft boil. Take the size of mozzarella ball you would like to make into your gloved hands and quickly dip the cheese down into the water. Begin to stretch it and then form it back into a ball. It will get shiny. You don't want to over do it. Just use the hot water to help form the cheese. Set each piece off to the side as you are finished.

Once every piece as been shaped (the size is up to you) place them into a cool bath of lightly salted water for 15–25 minutes. Too much salt for too long will cause a thick skin on your cheese. You can store your cheese in olive oil or plain in the refrigerator for about two weeks if it will last that long in your house. It lasts one evening here.

Dressed Eggs

-Oeufs Mayonnaise

This is a quintessential Midwestern hors d'oeuvre, and though most people equate this dish with a cook out, arranged on a plate with a small salad and a glass of wine, you've made yourself a delightful luncheon or light dinner. The creamy mayonnaise makes this a decadent and satisfying meal when you are watching your waistline.

You will need:
6 eggs
¼ cup of mayonnaise (see page 46)
2 tablespoons of white wine mustard
One handful of finely chopped fresh chives
Parsley and tarragon
Finely chopped red onion
Sea salt and pepper to taste
Capers (optional)

For perfectly hard-boiled eggs, place eggs in a saucepan and cover with cold water. Cook over high heat until the water begins to simmer. Turn off the heat, cover with a lid and allow to rest for seventeen minutes. While eggs are resting combine the mayonnaise, mustard, salt and pepper in a separate bowl. When the eggs are ready, drain the hot water; rinse the eggs with ice-cold water and peel. Carefully cut eggs lengthwise and remove the yolks, putting them in a separate bowl. Gently break up the egg yolks and then fold them into the mustard mixture. Using a pastry bag or spoon fill the halved eggs.

Finely chop a handful of parsley, chives, tarragon and red onion and sprinkle over the eggs.

Bon appétit!

From France to the Farm

Fried Potato Omelet
-omelette frite aux pommes de terre

To save time I make my omelets a good size and then divide them up between the family. Or, if we've been in the gardens and "farming" all day then, the menfolk and those growing girls ask for their own. These are truly humble acre omelets with eggs from our "ladies," herbs and potatoes from our potager and chèvre from our beloved dairy goats: Coco (Chanel) and Carolina (Herrera). *Mais bien sûr*... the goats are named after fashion designers.

Whether you find your ingredients at the farmers market, the super market or your own back forty you will beam with pride at the simple deliciousness of this meal.

To make an individual omelet you will need:
2 eggs, beaten
1 Yukon gold potato
2 ½ inch slices of chèvre
Herbes de Provence
Sea salt and cracked pepper to taste
Butter or goose fat to grease the skillet

Slice the potato into ¼ inch slices and fry in butter or goose fat until golden or crispy depending on your preference. Set aside.

In a small bowl beat two eggs and add the Herbes de Provence, salt and pepper, all to taste.

In a medium sized skillet melt the butter or goose fat.

Fry the potato slices until golden or crispy, depending on your preference and set aside. In a small bowl beat the eggs and mix in the Herbes de Provence, sea salt and pepper. Melt the butter or goose fat in a medium sized skillet and pour the beaten eggs onto the skillet. Tilt the skillet side to side, if necessary, to spread the eggs throughout. As the eggs begin to cook, carefully flip the omelet, either with a spatula or by flipping the mixture by jutting the skillet forward causing the omelet to flip itself. (It takes some practice but it's lots of fun!). Once the omelet is gently cooked, promptly remove it from the heat source and place the potatoes and chèvre in the center and fold the left side over the right. Serve immediately.

The recipe should be multiplied to accommodate the amount of servings needed. If you are preparing for a large group (like me!) when you are finished cooking the omelet place it on a piece of parchment paper and put another piece on top, preparing it for the next omelet. Once all the omelets are made you can assemble them and serve. For additional flavor you can add bacon, sautéed spinach and or a bit of raspberry jam.

Ambrosia

-Chantilly

Ambrosia, it's simply a lovely name for whipped crème and we use a lot of it around our kitchen. A dollop on our coffee over the weekends or a little on the side of a very chocolatey dessert. You can add a variety of liquors for different flavors and we love to add a tablespoon of high quality balsamic vinegar for an amazing dip for strawberries!

You will need:
1 pint of heavy cream
3-4 tablespoons of powdered sugar
1 egg white (This is a trick from my Great Gramma and it prevents the whipped cream from separating and turning runny when refrigerated.)

With your stand mixer or hand mixer mix whipping cream on high with the powdered sugar. When peaks begin to form mix in the egg white until thoroughly blended.

Optional flavors:
2 tablespoons of liqueur of choice
Or
2 tablespoons of high quality balsamic vinegar

Parisienne Farmgirl Hint: For a true, French Chantilly taste add one tablespoon of Kirsch.

Sugared Eggs
-oeufs sucrés

Straight from the kitchen of my Great Gramma. She served these with fried potatoes and fresh radishes. This is a farmgirl recipe if there ever was one.

You will need:
3 eggs
1 level tablespoon of sugar
Milk
3 heaping tablespoons of flour

Using a regular tablespoon from the silverware drawer (not a measuring spoon), measure three heaping spoonful's of flour and one spoonful of sugar and mix them together in a small bowl. Add enough milk to make the flour and the sugar become pasty. Add the eggs and stir well. Add more milk to make it runny (runnier than pancake batter). Pour into a hot skillet and cook over medium-low heat, uncovered until it is bubbly and solid enough to be flipped. Carefully flip it over and finish cooking through. Spoon into serving dish or bowl and sprinkle with a little additional sugar.

The Simple Life

When we look back to how our rural Grammas and Great Grammas lived we see an idealized, simple life, don't we? But if we look close enough, we see that it was a home-centered life where survival was the priority. The narcissism of today's world, that luxury of being the center of the universe, wasn't available to them, and they were better people for it. From the outside looking in... or into the past as it were, it appears as though the family was the social structure for the community. Each family member played a vital role in the success of the families survival.

I love to ask my Grandparents about what their everyday life was like: the little things, the meals, the chores, the family dynamics, and in their answers I find the little gems to apply to my own inspiration for the simple life. Their answers charm me and I find myself most touched about how their answers revolve around two things: their parents and food.

I am most grieved when I see how today's children seem so disconnected from the center of the family. Part of our goals when moving to our little farm was that this life and its responsibilities would bind our family together as a team. There is an annual cycle of work that we've come to know. In the winter we pour over seed catalogs and plan out our garden, celebrating in advance the meals to come. On April 15th we dig trenches and we plant potatoes together. In the summer we butcher our chickens, and in the fall we welcome baby goats. When my children look back on their own stories of days gone by, whether they be profound or simple, I hope they recall a family life free from empty distractions and free from the turmoil of an over-scheduled calendar. The simple life.

In assembling this book I had the opportunity to pick my dear Gramma's brain as to what her most profound memories are. I was anxious to hear about her time with her mother in the kitchen and in the garden, as that is where I spend most of my time with my own daughters. Great Gramma was known for serving many, many people food each weekend. There are stories of her cooking for thirty and forty people at a time, which sort of makes my job of cooking for seven a little easy!

Saturday morning would be her time to bake for the weekend and coming week. As I had to clean the upstairs bedrooms I could hear her singing down in the kitchen as she baked. Two songs I remember were "You are My Sunshine" and "Detour, There's a Muddy Road Ahead" plus many hymns that she knew.

I often imagine my Gramma as a little girl with her gorgeous jet-black hair and tomboy ways (she had many brothers!) running around my Great Gramma's skirts at the cook stove.

In the wintertime I would have to fill the cob box by the old cook stove. We had a room in the basement that we stored the cobs in from the corn sheller my Dad had.

I remember going to basement to get the butter that was in a jar sitting on a brick in the Artesian well that flowed constantly. That was how we kept things cold before we had a refrigerator.

I've asked both my Grandparents about this system of keeping things cool before the icebox was around. They described this "Artesian well" as a shallow well down in the cellar that was about 8 inches deep and flowed with constant ice-cold water. Thinking about this fills me with wonder! I can't help but ponder, how were they dug? How were they found? Actually, my Grampa tells a story of an Indian coming to the farm when we was a little boy. He was a "water witcher" (The method is also sometimes referred to as Water Dowsing or Willow Witching) and he walked slowly along with two sticks extended forward and once they crossed and formed an "x" that indicated that there was water below and a well was dug. Incredible.

Each year we would can peaches, pears and apples and red cherries (we had our own cherry tree). Mom and I also canned green beans, corn and potatoes and beef. We would also make our own sausage and hand soap.

I recently stumbled upon an incredible find for our hard cider making here on the farm: a cast iron fruit press and sausage maker. It appears to date from about 1889 and when I called my Gramma via the wonderful and oh-so-modern Facetime and showed her my latest cast iron conquest she said, "Yeap, that's exactly what we used to make our sausage with." As I hung up the phone I felt like had captured a piece of cast-iron family history!

Every spring and fall we carried all the rugs and mattresses outside for airing and a good beating, turned them over and beat them again. As we would carry the mattresses back upstairs, we would get the giggles and loose all our strength and have to stop in the middle of the stairs and settle down. All anybody would have to say is "done get the giggles" what fun memories!!!

It's easy for families to forget the importance of working together. We live in a consumer- and entertainment-focused world, but what a gift we give our children when we teach them to work. When we prepare a home-grown, from-scratch meal, my children get to experience the full circle of the fruits of our labor. As I watch my children out in the barnyard at chore time, I pray they are storing up memories. We've chosen this homesteading way of life. We're not aiming for easy; we've come to learn that delicious food tastes even that much better with a side of dirty hands and the sweat of our brow. We wouldn't have it any other way.

Detour, there's a muddy road ahead.
Detour, paid no mind to what it said.
Detour, all these bitter things I find.
Should have read that detour sign.

On Vintage Aprons

142 Parisienne FARMGIRL

I love buying them, old, stiff and starched to the nines.

I love making my own starch and pressing mine, patiently with a fire-hot iron.

I love the motherly feeling they give me when I wear them.

And I love when my little ones ask to wear one, too.

I don't know when I fell in love with aprons. Probably right about the time I started to bake bread and realized wiping my flour-covered hands on dark denim jeans was a no-go. The obsession really started for me one afternoon at my friends' resale shop when I scored a whole pile of them. Since then I have been known to rummage through stacks of linens in the forgotten corners of antique stores or the cardboard boxes that line a driveway during a garage sale… searching for the perfect apron to add to my collection.

My mom says that my Great Gramma always had an apron on, with seeds in the pocket. I can see how that would happen. Don't let mine fall to the floor for seeds spill out just about every time.

There is simply something about them. Something that says to me, "Momma is here. She is here to serve, here to take care of you." or "Momma means business, she's got her apron on." They are so feminine and so homey. I'm pretty short-waisted so they are not that flattering, but dang, they sure are cute.

If you come over and I am in the kitchen, chances are you'll find me with an apron on. If I invite you over to cook or bake with me, I'll most likely offer you one.

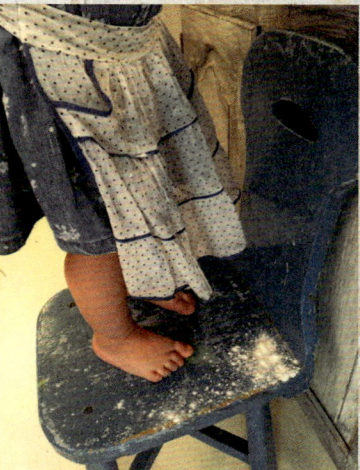

And then, there is the ceremony of removing the apron to sit down and finally dine.

I love that.

From France to the Farm

On Table Flowers

From France to the Farm • 145

Herb Bouquet

-bouquet garni

Just blocks from my little 17-meter-squared apartment in Paris was a new little shop that opened during my brief time living there. I will never forget the shopkeeper. He was very nervous at his grand opening and hungry for success. He sold all sorts of simple culinary must-haves from delicious tins of *foie gras* to walnut oil with floating walnuts visible thru the glass (I bought one of those and though it is long rancid, I cannot bring myself to throw it out). He sold wonderful toothpaste-style tubes of mustard, and bottles of wine, champagne, olives, vinegars and little bags of *bouquet garni*. I took three bags of tiny *bouquet garni* home with me and sparingly used them until I realized I could grow my own.

Simply put a *bouquet garni* is a bundle of aromatic herbs. Sometimes packed in a little bag that is easily hung off the side of your pot, other times bound with kitchen twine or leek leaves ready to be thrown into the pot to add heady flavor and fished out when the cooking is over.

In my kitchen I make and use two kinds of *bouquet garni*, growing everything in my herb garden except the bay leaf. I tie both varieties (both French and Italian) together with a long leek leaf.

You can grow your own or purchase fresh herbs at your local market. Simply make bunches with the herbs below or combination of your choice, leave them to dry on a cooling rack used for baking or hang them from some more twine with clothespins. Once they are dry you can store them in a sealed, plastic bag to use throughout the year.

Provençal Blend

Rosemary
Italian Parsley
Thyme
Bay Leaf
Sage

Italian Blend

Italian Parsley
Rosemary
Bay Leaf
Basil
Oregano

On Half-Way Farm We Grow

Rosemary
Thyme
Black Opal Basil
Lemon Thyme
Sage
Variegated Sage
Sweet Basil
Thai Basil
Lemon Balm
Chamomile
Ladies Mantle
Cilantro
Parsley
Sweet Mint
Peppermint
Greek Oregano
Lavender

Vegetable and Herb Pairings

While not exactly precise recipes, here is a small sampling of the hundreds of different ways you can bring your vegetable dishes to life by using herbs.

Carrots can be paired with sage, thyme, chives, basil and parsley. For a more exotic touch try curry, cinnamon, ginger, nutmeg and even coconut.

Cauliflower goes well with so many spices and herbs. In fact, cauliflower will often take on the flavor of whatever you are cooking it with which is why people use it these days for substitute mashed potatoes or faux pizza crust. It's excellent when enhanced with dill, basil and of course, nutmeg. Steamed and drizzled with a quality olive oil and enhanced with tarragon or thyme and you have a lovely side dish or vegetarian main course.

Zucchini is often found in abundance in the garden and so experimenting with new ways to prepare it is vital. Garlic, basil, oregano and parsley can be used... and of course... chocolate!

Broccoli is a staple in the spring garden and when combined with rosemary, marjoram, nutmeg and sage you get to experience it many different ways. I like to sauté mine in a skillet with butter, spring chives and their purple, peppery flowers.

Asparagus season is a special time of year. This early spring delight is hungered for by many all winter long. Making a special butter sauce with tarragon and chives is a simple way to enjoy these favorite spears. Try a puff pastry with some Émmental cheese, salt, pepper and nutmeg for a delicious dish.

Leeks are my favorite. They are so easy to grow and though surely the food of peasants in ages past, they add vegetable sophistication to any dish as the gourmet star of the onion family. Think braised leeks, sautéed leeks, leeks in chicken potpie and leeks in soups. They are a must-have for any potager and are paired well with bay leaves, dill, thyme and Dijon mustard.

Green beans are perfection alone so they don't need to many herbs to be delicious. Garlic, shredded basil leaves, and peppercorns. Simply fold your selected herb into your prepared green beans with some quality butter *et voilà!*

Potatoes are the vegetable of any true Farmgirl or Parisienne. Give me a potato and a trip to my herb garden and I'll make you a meal. Garlic, pepper, rosemary, rosemary and more rosemary, thyme and nutmeg, especially when using heavy, cream or cheese) will make even the most humble potato the star of your meal!

Tomatoes are almost instinctively paired with herbs. Basil is a tomatoes best friend. The two are excellent for co-planting and together on a plate. Other herbs that get a chance to shine with tomatoes are cilantro, dill, oregano, parsley, rosemary and pepper.

Radish are a family favorite and since I always plant too many, it's important for me to try preparing them in new ways before they go to waste. Radishes can be paired with arugula, basil, Romano cheese and a touch of olive oil for a refreshing springtime salad. Other herbs that add even more punch to radishes are borage, chives, mint and parsley.

Peas scream for herbs. I love *les petit pois* and love to play with chives, dill, mint, nutmeg, rosemary and chervil. A touch of cream and some butter and you can't go wrong.

You will notice that different meats have different strengths and weaknesses. Herbs play an incredible role in downplaying those weaknesses and accenting those strengths. The key is to learn which meats may need a little help and which meats can take all the boldness you can afford them.

Chicken is not a high fat meat, but fat is something that really brings out the flavor in a meat dish. When preparing chicken you want to consider which herbs can act as a flavor substitute for that missing fat. Rosemary is a bold, piney herb that pairs well with the weakness of chicken. Garlic adds that missing flavor too. Garlic is a favorite in our chicken dishes here on the farm. Tarragon, marjoram, dill, parsley, thyme and coriander work as well. Simply lift the skin and sprinkle on the meat before laying the skin back down and sprinkle inside the chicken cavity when baking a chicken.

When preparing a pork dish, I like to highlight the meats earthy flavor. The earthiest of herbs is sage but your "seed herbs" like fennel, caraway, and fennel are earthy too. Seasoning the meat with these dried herbs or rubbing the meat with fresh herbs is beneficial. Other herbs that compliment pork's unique flavor are bay leaf, cardamom, ginger, thyme and tarragon.

Bloodier meats like beef and venison bring a ton of flavor to the table so they can handle a ton of flavor in return! When making your steaks, pot roast and venison dishes feel confident and slather on all that Mother Nature will allow. Garlic, rosemary, chives, thyme, tarragon, parsley will all serve your red meat dishes well. While you're at it bring forth the butter and the high quality olive oil and make your red meat incredible!

Meat and Herb Pairings

From France to the Farm • 157

Herbed Butter

-beurre aux herbes

Midwest winters are long, grey and colorless. I rather hate them, but alas, I am a Midwest girl and Lake Michigan runs through my veins. The months of gray cause the gardeners heart to ache and I crave the greens of herbs and the vibrant blue sky of the gardening season. I look for ways to recreate the excitement of that first day I get to play in the dirt.

The brilliant green of the herbs preserved in this butter does that for me. The hearty, earthy flavor gets me excited about another year of gardening to come, not to mention the food on my plate. So go ahead. How about some herb butter? Seed planting is just around the corner.

This recipe makes 8 ounces or feel free to duplicate and freeze the extras.

You will need:
½ pound of salted butter
Two cups of fresh herbs

I choose sage, parsley, chives, thyme and a little rosemary but you can also enhance your butter with shallots, garlic and whatever else you stumble upon in your herb garden.

If chilled, allow the butter to just about reach room temperature. Wash your herbs and allow them to dry and pulse them in your food processor until they are uniform in size. Add the butter and continue to pulse until well blended. Refrigerate in a glass container or freeze in a plastic bag. I press mine towards the bottom of the bag to make the shape of a goat cheese like log and then I roll the bag, eliminating any extra air before sealing.

This is an excellent way to use up any remaining herbs in your garden at the end of the season. You know that night before the first hard frost? I make up as many batches as I can and store them in freezer to enjoy all winter long.

All Things Farine

Shortcrust
-pâte brisée

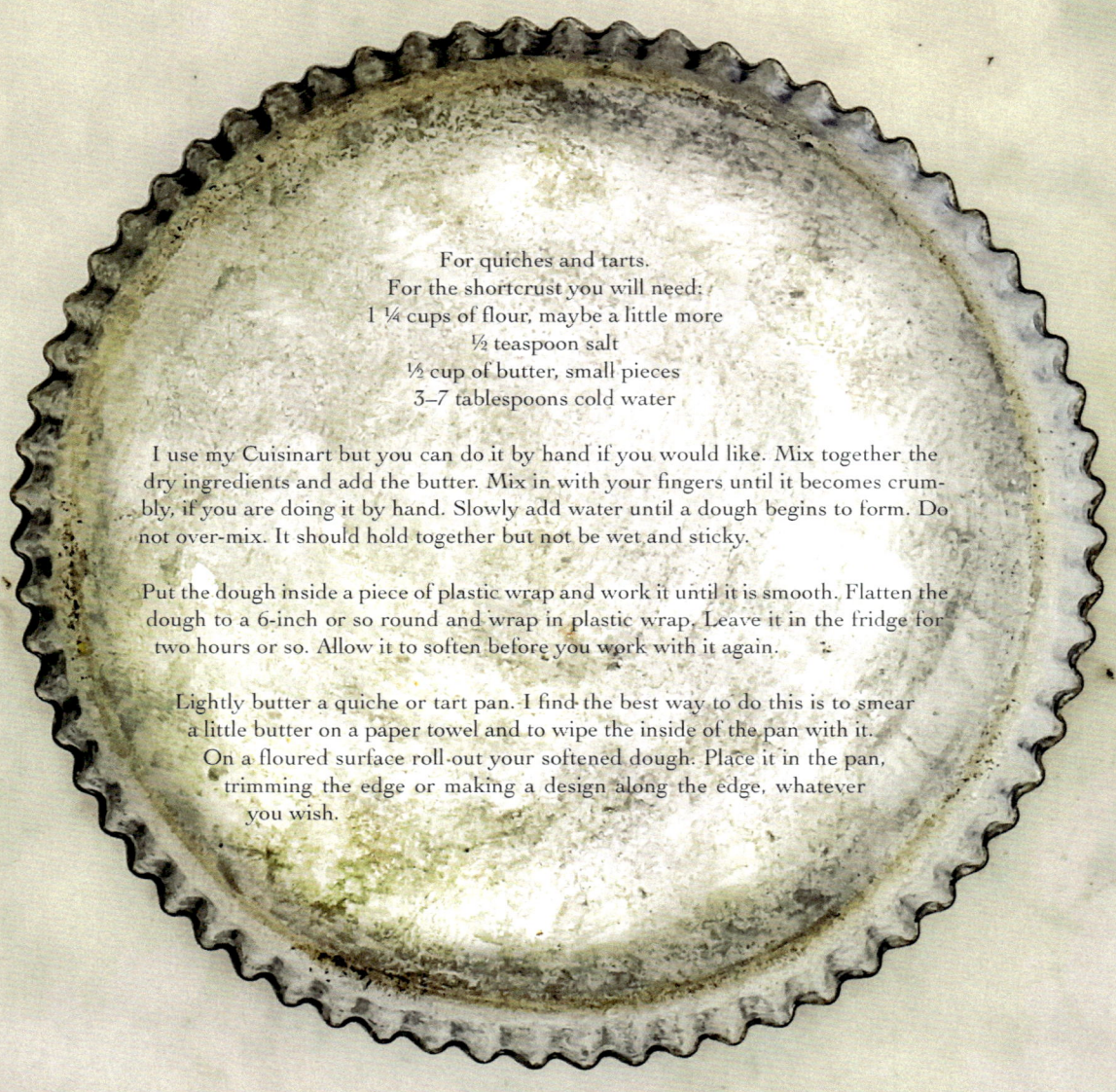

For quiches and tarts.
For the shortcrust you will need:
1 ¼ cups of flour, maybe a little more
½ teaspoon salt
½ cup of butter, small pieces
3–7 tablespoons cold water

I use my Cuisinart but you can do it by hand if you would like. Mix together the dry ingredients and add the butter. Mix in with your fingers until it becomes crumbly, if you are doing it by hand. Slowly add water until a dough begins to form. Do not over-mix. It should hold together but not be wet and sticky.

Put the dough inside a piece of plastic wrap and work it until it is smooth. Flatten the dough to a 6-inch or so round and wrap in plastic wrap. Leave it in the fridge for two hours or so. Allow it to soften before you work with it again.

Lightly butter a quiche or tart pan. I find the best way to do this is to smear a little butter on a paper towel and to wipe the inside of the pan with it. On a floured surface roll out your softened dough. Place it in the pan, trimming the edge or making a design along the edge, whatever you wish.

Chamomile and Lavender French Toast

-pain perdu à la camomille et à la lavande

You will need:
3 cups of flour
4 eggs
4 cups of milk
1 cup of sugar, divided
1 teaspoon of salt
2 tablespoons Bourbon vanilla
2 tablespoons baking powder
4 tablespoons loose, dried chamomile flowers, divided
4 tablespoons dried lavender buds (could use fresh lavender buds if needed)
Sliced bread
Sunflower oil for frying

My routine in the kitchen...*à la cuisine* is a earthy, organic, romantic one when I am in the zone. Romantic movie soundtracks play in my mind and the artist inside awakens with an overwhelming desire to give my family warm, fond memories of Momma's food around the table. When the spirit moves, it's often a walk thru my potager and herb garden for inspiration.

This summer we overslept for church and had a quiet morning to ourselves without the hustle of having to get out the door, and I wanted to do something lovely for my family with the few extra hours we had. I had just finished drying out my chamomile harvest. The lavender was in full, abundant swing and a full bottle of maple syrup in the pantry was beckoning.

I made a full pot of coffee and told everyone to give me about twenty minutes. I promised to make it worth the wait.

It was.

Chamomile can be found in little spice bags in the ethnic aisle of many grocery stores and both dried lavender and chamomile can easily be ordered online. Why not have them on hand for your next cup of tea or for that morning you decide to experiment in your own kitchen.

In a mixing bowl or stand mixer combine the milk, eggs, vanilla and ½ cup of the sugar. Add the flour, salt, baking powder, lavender and two tablespoons of the chamomile. Blend until mix thoroughly.

In a shallow soup bowl mix the remaining sugar and chamomile flowers.

In a large cast iron skillet heat one inch of sunflower oil until it is hot enough for frying. Slightly remix batter, as lavender will have floated to the surface. Dunk bread slices in the batter and fry on each side until golden brown. With tongs remove them from the skillet and drag them through the sugar/chamomile blend to coat them. Allow them to drain on a paper towel lined plate.

Serve with butter and maple syrup. This recipe makes enough to serve 6 people and refrigerate remaining batter for later in the week. Can be halved.

Cinnamon Rolls

-petits pains à la cannelle

For the rolls you will need:
8 cups of flour
4 eggs
2 cups of milk
1 cup of warm water
5 teaspoons of yeast
1 cup of butter, divided, melted
½ cup & 1 tablespoon of sugar, divided
1 teaspoons of salt
Extra cinnamon and sugar to shake over dough

These cinnamon rolls are another fine example of my extraordinary Great Gramma. Though I only know of the stories of her kitchen abilities. She had sadly gone blind and needed care by the time I was a young child. I know now, as a woman with small children underfoot in the kitchen, that to pull off the quantities of homemade food that she made on a weekly, if not daily, basis meant she had to be some kind of woman! Make these for your family and I promise, they'll be calling you "some kind of a woman!" too.

Makes about two dozen rolls.

In a sauce pan, scald the milk by heating it on medium heat until it begins to bubble around the edge of the pan. In a separate bowl mix together warm water, yeast and 1 tablespoon of the sugar. Set aside, it will rise a little. After milk has cooled add ½ of cup butter, the remaining ½ cup sugar, salt and eggs. Combine water mixture and milk mixture, add flour, one cup at a time until mixed well. Let it rise for two hours then roll out to about ¼ inch thick (You will want to flour your surface before rolling). Preheat oven to 350 degrees. Melt the remaining butter and pour over the rolled out dough. Spread butter all over the dough with a basting brush. Sprinkle cinnamon and sugar all over the melted butter and gently roll into one long roll. With a knife or dough scraper cut into 1 ½ to 2 inch slices. Place in pie pans or casserole dishes. Allow them to rise for another hour and then bake until golden brown. Do not over bake.

For the frosting you will need:
½ cup of butter
3 cups of powdered sugar
2–5 tablespoons of milk to create the consistency of frosting you prefer.

Mix in food processor or with hand mixer. Spread on rolls just before they are completely cooled.

Unfrosted rolls can be frozen for up to four months. Frost before serving.

I double and triple this recipe every fall and freeze them to have them ready for cold, winter mornings when we need a treat. These rolls are also a lovely for company or for a friend who's spread a little thin.

I double and triple this recipe every fall and freeze them to have them ready for cold, winter mornings when we need a treat. These rolls are also lovely for company or for a friend who's spread a little thin.

Half-Way Burger Buns
-petits pains pour hamburger façon ferme à mi-chemin

If bad shoes ruin an outfit (and trust me, they do) then a store bought bun is going to ruin your Half-Way Hamburger. These buns are everything they should be: sweet, dense and filling. Why not make extra and freeze them for your next cookout? Makes 12–14 large buns. I use my stand mixer for this recipe.

You will need:
7 cups of flour
4 tablespoons of yeast
2 ¼ cups warm water
½ cup melted coconut oil or olive oil
½ cup sugar
2 eggs
2 teaspoons salt

In a mixing bowl combine the yeast and water. Mix to dissolve. Add the sugar and oil and let it rest for a couple of minutes. Add the eggs & salt. Oil will have separated a bit. Remix. Add the flour little by little using the mixing attachment. When all the flour has been added knead for five minutes on a floured surface until the dough is smooth. Form into 12–14 small rounds. Cover with a flour sack towel for eight minutes. Bake for 12–15 minutes or until lightly browned.

Parisienne Farmgirl hint:
After your burgers have cooked you can scrape any remaining meat off the grill rack or your cast iron skillet. Lightly butter the inside of your sliced hamburger buns and cook them, briefly, butter side down. Thy will become crispy and even more delicious than before! You'll never want a restaurant burger again!

Dinner Biscuits

-petits pains

Let's face it, when I make biscuits it is almost always in some sort of dinner-time emergency where I have thrown a soup together because groceries are low. When I bust out the biscuits with a homemade jam from the cupboard or herb butter my family "oo's and ah's" and no one suspects my Mother Hubbard-esque situation.

These are easy. No rolling or cutting. In fact, I usually give my little girls the task of making these for me and they love it. This recipe makes a ton of biscuits and can easily be divided.

You will need:
10 cups of flour
3 teaspoons of salt
4 tablespoons of baking powder
⅔ cup of cold butter
4 cups of cold milk

Preheat the oven to 450 degrees. Mix everything together (except the cold milk) in stand mixer, just enough to cut in the butter. Transfer to a large mixing bowl or your stand mixer and add the milk little by little until just blended. If you are not using a stand mixer use your hand or a wooden spoon to mix in the milk. Shape into large, loose rounds and place on parchment paper on a baking tray. Bake for 8–12 minutes or until tips have begun to golden.

Serve with jam, honey, herb butter or your favorite topping.

Classic French Pancakes
-crêpes traditionnelles

We sat there on a green bench, shaded by the most ancient church in the city, with hot crêpes in hand and watched with amusement as a beautiful young *Parisienne* pulled up with an aim to parking her little car in the even littler space before us. We smiled and raised our eyebrows at her bold intentions, and she looked at us with an expression as if to say, "I got this." Back and forth she went, bumping the car in front of her and the car behind repeatedly, until she had parked her six-foot long car in the five-foot space in front of our bench there on the Boulevard Saint-Germain.

Boulevard Saint-Germain des Prés and Rue Bonaparte, you could say that at this intersection is everything that epitomizes Paris: the ancient church of Saint-Germain des Prés, the chic Louis Vuitton, Les Deux Magot café, and in my opinion, the best crêpe stand in the city. You can smell them from across the street, your stomach hollow and feet aching from a day of sight seeing. They are made to order and absolutely delicious, and you can easily bring the taste home to your kitchen today. So turn on some Edith Piaf, *Sous le Ciel de Paris* and take yourself back... or with your imagination and taste buds, visit for the first time.

You will need:
1 cup of flour
¼ cup of sugar
¼ teaspoon of salt
3 eggs, beaten
1 cup of milk
3 tablespoons of butter, melted
Wax paper

Use a crêpe pan or skillet to melt the butter and set it aside. Sift the dry ingredients. Add the milk to the beaten eggs and add to the dry ingredients. Add the melted butter and blend with your electric mixer or whisk until completely smooth.

Reheat the crêpe pan or skillet, lined with the residual butter, to a medium heat. Add just enough batter to the skillet and tilt it back and forth so that it covers the entire skillet.

Using a spatula lift up the edge of the crêpe as it cooks. Once it looks light brown, flip it to cook the other side.

Place the cooked crêpe on the wax paper and prepare the next. Placing another sheet of wax paper on top of the crêpe and stack the next prepared crêpe on top. Continue in this fashion if preparing crêpes for many people or assemble as you go.

There are thousands of ways to prepare crêpes but these are two classic Paris street vendor crêpes:

Savory:
While your crêpe is cooking on the second side break an egg over the center and gently whisk it with a fork so it cooks to an over easy setting. Sprinkle the egg with Gruyere or Emmental cheese and optional diced ham. Add salt and pepper to taste and fold in half, and in half again. Enjoy!

Sweet:
While your crêpe is cooking on the second side, sprinkle Grand Marnier liquor over the top and follow with a sprinkling of sugar. Fold in half, and in half again. Try not to eat two!

Pizza Dough
-pâte à pizza

Sundays on our farm are for church, NASCAR and gardening. I grew up eating pot roast on Sundays but... as for me and my family... we love homemade pizza on Sunday afternoons. Pizzas are a chance for the whole family to get involved. The children love to roll out the dough, sprinkle the herbs and cheese and spread the sauce. We gather our toppings in season or select them earlier in the week at the supermarket and then we snuggle up and watch our favorite drivers race for that checkered flag. Go Junior! Can I get an "Amen"?

You will need:
2/3 cup of lukewarm water
2 tablespoons of yeast
2 tablespoons of olive oil
2 cups of flour, a bit extra if your dough is too sticky
A pinch of salt
We are known to season our crust with dried oregano, dried basil, red pepper, etc.
Corn meal for preparing your pan

Preheat your oven to 450 degrees. Lightly oil a pizza pan or cookie sheet with olive oil and sprinkle with course corn meal. Enough to lightly cover the surface.

In your mixer or food processor combine the water and yeast. Add the remaining ingredients and roll out your pizza crust. For thin crust pizza you do not allow the dough to rise. For thicker crust allow the dough to rise.

To prepare the pan wipe it down with olive oil and sprinkle corn meal across. Carefully lift up the rolled out dough and place it on your prepared pan. Prick it a few times with a fork and back it for five minutes. Remove the pan from the oven and assemble your pizza. Put it back in the oven and continue to bake until your desired doneness. We like ours well done.

For extra crispy crust in the last few minutes of baking carefully slide the pizza off onto the oven racks and allow it to finish right on the rack. Use caution when sliding it back onto the tray for removal from the oven.

Basic Baguettes
-baguettes

My apartment in Paris was a ten-minute walk from one of Eric Kayser's Paris boulangeries. Every day that I could I would join his devotees and stand in line for a warm, crusty, dare I say, heavenly baguette. It was worth the wait and I would walk back to my little flat munching along the way. *M. Kayser's* baguettes are a science unto themselves. They are a source of inspiration for me to this day.

The ability to make a basic baguette is one that is worth the investment of time. There is a satisfaction that comes with the offering of a warm baguette to friends and family alike. Most Americans do not have the luxury of living within walking distance to a classic boulangerie so lucky for us we can set our expectations at a more realistic level. After many years of trying different techniques I am happy to make these until I have a proper bread oven and a better understanding of Eric Kayser's technique. For now though I think these do the trick.

This recipe makes two baguettes.

You will need:
3 cups of flour
½ teaspoon of yeast
1 ¾ teaspoon of salt
1 ⅓ cups of water

Additional flour for dusting

Combine all the ingredients in a large, stainless steel bowl and mix with a serving fork. Dough will be rough so be sure there is no dry flour residue hidden beneath what you have mixed. Cover the bowl securely with plastic wrap and allow to rise in a warm location for 12–18 hours.

After the rising time bring the dough to your work surface, divide it into two pieces and shape them very, very gently into two balls. Allow them to rest for ten minutes with the crease side down.

Take your first ball of dough and turn it smooth side down and flatten it a bit with the palm of your hand. Fold the right and left sides in to meet each other and secure together. It will be a slight rectangle. Continue this way with each ball of dough.

Take the piece of dough that you started with in the previous step and lay it smooth side down with the short sides being the right and left. Roll it towards you pressing with your thumbs throughout the motion then pinch the seams together. Allow to rest with the seam on top as you continue in this fashion with the other pieces.

Roll these pieces back and forth with your hand stretched out over them encouraging them to stretch in length.

Grease your baguette pans by oiling a paper towel and applying coconut or olive oil to it. Rub your pans down and transfer your loaves. Return them a warm location (like the top of your refrigerator) for another 1 ½ hours.

Dust your loaves with a little flour. With a serrated knife make slashes on the top of the baguettes on the diagonal. If your dough does not have much spring to it do not make deep cuts. The more spring it has the deeper the cut you can make. These cuts are not simply for aesthetic purposes. These cuts will help the loaf expand in the oven. It is easy to forget that you have bread rising. If your loaves have collapsed from letting them rise too long the combination of the cuts and a very hot and moist oven may save them.

When your dough is at the end of its rise, pre-heat your oven to 450 degrees. Place a small cast iron or oven-proof pan on a rack that will be empty once your bread is inside. When you are ready to bake your bread place your bread pan in the oven and throw a couple of ice cubes in the cast iron pan that has preheated with your oven. It will generate a lot of steam. Quickly close the door and begin baking. This steam is important, along with the high heat to imitate a commercial oven and will create excellent, crusty baguettes.

Serve your baguettes at the temperature of your choice. Once cooled they can be stored in zip-lock bags for a couple of days or frozen for a couple of months. To enjoy after freezing, thaw on counter for a couple of hours and re-bake at 275 degrees until warm.

Amélie's Honey Wheat Bread

-pain de blé au miel

I love to make bread.

There is something so homey about it, and it thrills my children. When Amélie was two she began calling my honey wheat "Homebread," and the name stuck.

When she was three years old we ran out of flour, and Joel ran to the store and bought a loaf of store bought whole wheat bread. I rudely scoffed aloud, disgusted at the myriad of chemical ingredients as he set it in the counter. A few days later Amélie gave her two cents on the situation, "I love Homebread, Mom. Some people buy their bread from the store... can you believe people eat that crap everyday?"

Feel free to pick yourself up off the floor.

Lord knows, I had to.

You will need:
3 cups warm of water or whey
5 teaspoons or 2 packages of active dry yeast
1 cup of honey, divided
5 cups of bread flour
3 tablespoons of butter, melted
1 tablespoon of salt
3 to 3 ½ cups of whole-wheat flour.
(Can substitute white wheat for a different style bread)

Mix the warm water, yeast, and ½ cup of the honey.

Add 5 cups of the white bread flour and stir to combine. Let it set for 30 minutes and it will become big and bubbly.

Mix in the melted butter and the remaining honey, and salt. Stir in 2 cups of whole-wheat flour. Mix until just combined and knead until just pulling away from the surface but sticky to touch. This may take an additional 1 – 1 ½ cups of whole-wheat flour. Place in a greased bowl, turning once to coat the surface of the dough. Cover with a dishtowel. Let it rise in a warm place until doubled.

Punch down, and divide into 3 loaves. Place in greased 9 x 5 inch loaf pans. Allow to rise until the dough has topped the pans by at least one inch.

Bake at 350 degrees for 25 to 30 minutes. You can optionally brush the tops of loaves with 2 tablespoons melted butter when done to prevent crust from getting hard.

This recipe is easily doubled and can be made by hand or with a stand mixer and bread hook.

Homemade Pasta
-pâtes faites maison

Sometimes I wonder if you ever lived until you've had your own address in Paris... experienced life on a farm... or eaten homemade pasta. I highly recommend all of those things of course but making homemade pasta is the easiest of the three.

I bought pasta attachments for my mixer last year, and the girls and I are completely addicted to making our own noodles. The rest of the family is positively spoiled and now they complain if I make pasta from a box.

Donnez-moi un break!

You may find that you need to tweak my recipe. I am NOT a big "measurer" so I leave some things to the eye. Trust yourself. **It's just pasta** — it's not a chocolate soufflé.

This is the base recipe that I used for all of our favorite pasta dishes. You will need a mixer with a pasta attachment but I'll bet you're smart enough to figure out how to make it with a manual pasta maker. I'll bet you can roll it out with your favorite rolling pin too!

You will need:
3–3 ½ cups of white flour
4 of the best eggs you can get your hands on
2 tablespoons of high quality olive oil
3–6 tablespoons of water
1 teaspoon of salt
Optional
For a pepper pasta you will need lots of homemade flower pepper (see page 41)

Mix your eggs in a small bowl and put your flour in your mixer's bowl. Add your eggs, salt and pepper to the flour and mix just slightly. Use your basic mixing attachment — the one that looks like a peace sign. Add olive oil and then the water, adding the water tablespoon by tablespoon. Mix it a bit... I count to thirty. You don't want the dough to be watery, but you don't want it dry and dusty either. It's not a perfect dough as it may be slightly crumbly at first. I personally don't care to work with it if it's terribly dry. If I find it too dry I add a tiny splash of olive oil.

As you make your pasta more frequently you will get the feel for what you like. You may want to add more olive oil, less water or visa versa. Switch to your dough hook and mix for a couple minutes. Two or so. Don't over mix.

You will then remove the dough and form it into a ball. Get your muscles ready and knead it on a floured counter top, as the gluten does its thing your dough will get smoother and easier to handle. Keep working it! Place it in a zip lock bag and let it sit for 20–30 minutes. No longer.

After the allowed time, divide it into four pieces.

Take one chunk and leave the others in the (slightly opened) zip lock so they don't begin to dry out. Form the first piece into a sort of rectangle about 5x3 inches. And now the fun part.

Install your lasagna attachment and set it to setting number 1. Turn on your mixer and begin to feed your dough through. If your piece is about a half inch thick it should grab, if it won't grab you may want to flatten one of the three-inch sides of your rectangle so it does. Just give it a little pinch along the edge so it will catch in the rollers. Run the piece through one time and then fold it in half. Run it through one or two more times. Each time your dough is going to become more and more compliant. Dust very lightly with flour in between each step.

Next switch the setting on the attachment to level two and run your dough through once or twice. Continue in this fashion until you have run it through twice on level four. This is my preferred thickness. Stopping at level three makes fine noodles, too. Just look at the thickness of your dough and determine if you want to keep going. I like a hearty noodle but you may want to continue to level five or even six. You can have the speed on your mixer set on two so that it doesn't take all evening. At this point you will have a flat piece of pasta that is 24–36 inches in length. Lay your dough out on a flour dusted surface and repeat this process with your next three pieces.

Now, you will want to attach your desired noodle attachment. Make sure your big, flat noodle is lightly dusted and run that piece through, holding the right side up. If you let it hang the pasta will stop feeding through because of the weight of the dough.

Hang your noodles to dry and promptly use or store in a sealed bag. You can also make little pasta nests and freeze the nests for future use. I advise dusting your noodles thoroughly as they are drying or before freezing.

From France to the Farm • 181

Apple Ricotta Pancakes

-crêpes au fromage ricotta et aux pommes

Pancakes are a morning staple in my kitchen, and they sometimes they bail me out for dinner too! I'm greeted with squeals of delight as five little ones come bounding down the stairs. I crank up all four burners and use every bit of cast iron I can get my hands on so that I can make as many as possible at a time.

I have my own memories of bounding down my Gramma's farmhouse stairway to the smell of bacon grease and pancakes. I can just see her standing there flipping away, ready to serve. She had been awake long before the rest of us. Though we've both aged since those days when she cooked for all of us like that, I still remember one rule: Gramma... or now Momma gets the last pancake. The last one tastes the best.

Mornings are intense for us on the farm. There are animal chores, music lessons, morning school and when we sit down for breakfast we are *hungry*. The children love it when I make pancakes and so to keep things interesting, I have tried to add variety to my basic recipe. These pancakes are so good. The ricotta gives them a depth to their flavor and the granny smiths stay crisp through the cooking process.

You will need:
2 cups of flour
2 eggs
1 cup of Ricotta cheese (see page 127)
2 cups of milk
2-3 Granny Smith apples
1 teaspoon of cinnamon
1 teaspoon vanilla
½ teaspoon of freshly ground nutmeg

Follow the Ricotta directions on page 127.

Peel the apples if you'd like. I love the texture of apple skin. Mix all ingredients together except the ricotta. When everything has been mixed, gently fold in the ricotta cheese.

Get out the cast iron if you have it! I fry my pancakes in either bacon grease or coconut oil.

Serve with piping hot coffee and *real* maple syrup. I mean come on, do I really need to say that?

Country Loaf
-pain campagnard

Our daily bread.

It may be more common for the French to rely on their local boulangerie for their daily bread however it is the tradition of the American farmer's wife to bake her own bread. It's our independent streak. How rogue and American of us!

This loaf is reminiscent of the artisan breads that French housewife might find in town, but now you can make it easily in your kitchen. The crumb and crunch will make you feel like a professional. If you make this while no one is home, be fair and try to save some for the others.

You will need:
6 cups of flour
2 ⅔ cups of warm water
1 tablespoon of yeast
1 ½ teaspoon salt

In a large bowl combine the water and yeast. Add the flour and salt and mix with a sturdy fork. I use a serving fork. The dough will have a rough, shaggy appearance. Mix thoroughly. Cover the bowl with plastic wrap and place in a warm area for eighteen hours.

After eighteen hours divide the dough into two pieces. Take each piece and fold it in half twice by folding it in half and then in half again. Cover loosely with the plastic wrap or with a fresh linen and allow the dough to rest for twenty minutes. Take each piece and gently form it into a ball (don't pack it tight, simply form it into a ball). Sprinkle your surface with flour or corn meal and rest the dough balls there for two hours, covering with a fresh linen.

Preheat the oven to 450 degrees. Thirty minutes before you bake your bread place your Dutch oven(s) in the oven to get them hot.

If you'd like you can dust the tops of your risen dough with additional flour or corn meal and with a sharp knife score them in the pattern of your choosing.

Gently slide your fingers underneath and carefully drop one into each Dutch oven. Shake the pan a little from side to side if your dough looks very lopsided.

Bake for about 25–30 minutes with the lid on the Dutch oven and then remove the lid for the final 10–15 minutes or until your bread is dark golden brown.

Your bread will sound hollow if tapped when it is done.

Brambleberries with Simple Custard

-mûres à la crème anglaise

Living on this little farm has brought many new adventures, like learning how to forage for food that grows on the property. Once we realized we could eat the thousands of berries growing in the brambles along the perimeter of our home, we felt like we had hit the jackpot. We picked, washed up, came right in and feasted like kings. Life on the farm got even better that day!

4 cups of whole milk
4 somewhat heaping tablespoons of cornstarch
¾ cup of organic sugar
1 vanilla bean
4 eggs, beaten

Beat eggs in a separate bowl. Set aside. Combine milk, sugar and cornstarch in your favorite saucepan and scald. Do not boil. Remove from heat and add ½ cup of milk mixture and the scraped out vanilla bean* to the eggs. Whisking. Slowly add egg/milk mixture back to the remaining milk mixture, reheat, whisking until it thickens. Add berries to top. Can be served hot, cold or room temp.

*Cut vanilla bean lengthwise, open and scrap out with an upsides down spoon.

Heavenly.

Gramma's Strawberry Shortcake

-tarte sablée aux fraise de grand-mère

My Gramma's CB name was "Strawberry" during their farming years. Back when she drove a red grain truck to the elevator in town or the pick up truck out to the fields with a front seat full of sandwiches and Pepsi's and sometimes a baby.

Back before cell phones and texting...

Strawberry, You got a copy?

Preheat your oven to 450 degrees.

Start with the best, sweetest strawberries you can find. Don't wash them until just before use. Gently strain, but don't allow them to become completely dry. After removing the tops, take a handful of berries. Put the strawberries into a shallow bowl and mash them with a fork, releasing the juices. A messy, haphazard sort of cut to release the juices. Add a bit of sugar and set them to the side. The sugar will draw out the juices and combine with the residual water while your oven heats.

You can also use this technique for freezing your berries.

You will need:
2 cups of flour
½ teaspoon of salt
4 teaspoons of baking powder
1 tablespoon of sugar
⅓ cup of lard
1 well-beaten egg
½ cup of milk

Combine the dry ingredients and lard and then fold in the egg and milk. Mix and form into small, biscuit sized rounds. Bake at 450 degrees until edges begin to turn golden.

For assembly you will need strawberries, really good vanilla ice cream, fresh cream or half & half and a biscuit.

Layer as you wish but you simply MUST pour the cream or Half & Half over everything. It mixes with the strawberry juice...

Oh-la-la!

Doubtless God could have made a better berry, but doubtless God never did.

Dr. William Butler, 17th century English writer

Queen of Sheba Cake
-reine de saba

This is my take on the traditional French cake called "Queen of Sheba." Like the Queen of Sheba probably was, this cake *is* luxurious. This cake makes a *fantastique* recipe to add to your repertoire. Dark chocolate, toasted almonds and amaretto make it a crowd pleaser. I love to give this cake as a gift, and I love to change the flavors to accommodate the recipient.

For the cake you will need:
2 cups of almond slivers, toasted
⅔ cup blanched almonds (I sometimes blanch my own but I LOVE Trader Joe's almond meal)
⅔ cup of super fine sugar
¼ cup of flour
½ cup unsalted butter
5 ounces semi-sweet chocolate (72% cacao), melted
3 eggs, separated
2 tablespoon of almond liqueur (Amaretto)

For the chocolate glaze you will need:
¾ cup of heavy cream or whipping cream
8 ounces of dark chocolate (I love to use 6 ounces of 72% and 2 ounces of 100%)
2 tablespoons of unsalted butter
2–3 tablespoons of almond liqueur

Preheat oven to 350 degrees. Heat a skillet on medium heat and toast the almond slivers until just browned. Put them into a bowl and set them aside. Prepare a nine-inch spring form pan with a parchment paper round. Lightly grease the pan and paper and dust with flour, tapping out any excess. Process the blanched almonds/almond meal and sugar in a food processor with a metal blade until very fine, transfer to a bowl and sift over the flour. Stir to mix and set aside. In another bowl mix the butter until creamy then add half of the sugar and beat for about 1–2 minutes until very light and creamy. In separate bowl, beat the egg whites until soft peaks form. Add the remaining sugar. Beat until they are stiff and glossy – I love that!!! Fold a quarter of the whites into the chocolate mixture to lighten it then alternately fold in the almond mixture and the remaining whites in three batches. Spoon the mixture into the prepared pan and spread evenly.

Bake in 350 degree oven for 30–35 minutes until the edge is puffed but the center is still soft and wobbly – a skewer inserted about 2 inches from the edge should come out clean. Transfer the cake in its pan to a wire rack or trivet. Allow to cool for 15 minutes, and then remove the sides. Invert the cake onto a 9-inch cake board and remove the base of the pan and paper.

To make the chocolate glaze, bring the cream to a boil in a saucepan. Remove from the heat and add the chocolate. Stir in gently until chocolate has melted and is smooth, then beat in the butter and liqueur. Cool for about 20–30 minutes until it has slightly thickened, stirring occasionally. Place the cake on a wire rack or if you don't have one, try an upside down bowl and a counter top lined with newspaper. Pour the warm chocolate glaze to cover the top completely. It may drip down on the sides; that's good, just take a spatula and add more to the sides of the cake to complete. Let it stand for a few minutes and then gently press the crushed almonds onto the sides of the cake. *Et voila!*

Parisienne Farmgirl hints:
If you choose to make your own almond meal simply blanch raw, unsalted almonds by boiling them for exactly one minute. Any more than 60 seconds could make them mushy. Strain immediately and rinse with cold water. Rub the almond in between your fingers. Skin will slid right off. Allow them to dry and blend them until they are almond flour in your food processor.

This cake can be made ahead of time and well wrapped will last in the fridge for 3 days.

Try making this cake and glaze with Framboise liqueur instead, skip the crushed almonds on the outside and line the top of the cake with Raspberries.

I have also made it with Grand Marnier and garnished with a candied orange slice.

Finished cake see page 188.

Hot Fudgy Pudding
-pudding chaud de fondant

Figure watching girls from an old, old, Bible study of mine called this dessert "Satan." I might argue instead that it's a bit of Heaven. I've been eating this since I was a wee-one, though these days I can only do one bowl lest I fall into a sugar-induced coma and not be able to do my farm chores.

There is still something so incredible about the fact that the dessert flip-flops while cooking. Almost as incredible as the crusty donut type cake that these simple ingredients make.

This recipe can be doubled. If doubling, use a 9x13" baking dish, otherwise use a 9"x9" baking dish.

Hold on to your socks. This one's going to go into your secret weapon arsenal.

You will need:
4 cups of flour
4 teaspoons of baking powder
2 teaspoons of salt
2/3 cup of sugar
8 tablespoons of melted butter
1 tablespoon of vanilla
2 cups of milk
8 tablespoons of dark, Dutch processed cooa
2 cups of brown sugar (see recipe page 35)
3 1/4 cups of boiling water

Preheat your oven to 350 degrees.

Combine flour, baking powder, salt, sugar, melted butter, vanilla and milk. Press as a layer covering the entire bottom of the baking dish. Bring the water to a boil in a separate sauce pan on the stovetop. In a separate bowl combine the brown sugar and cocoa then spread it evenly over the top of the flour mixture. Do not mix it in. Pull a rack from your preheated oven out about halfway. Place the baking dish on the rack and carefully pour the boiling water over the top. Carefully push the baking dish back in taking care not to spill any. I place a cookie sheet underneath to catch any boil over during baking. Helps keep your oven clean!

Serve hot with fresh Ambrosia (see recipe page 135)

Childhood Chocolate Cake

-gâteau au chocolat de mon enfance

This is the tried and true, quintessential chocolate cake recipe my mom would make us for our birthdays. I've only made one change — now it's a DARK chocolate cake. Because that's what makes my world right. Dark chocolate. I must insist that now that this recipe has come into your life that you will never, ever, ever purchase a boxed cake mix again. Ever.

For the cake you will need:
1 cup of soft butter
1 ¾ cup of sugar
1 tablespoon of vanilla
3 large eggs
1 cup of dark chocolate, Dutch processed cocoa
1 ¼ cups of unsifted flour
1 teaspoon of baking soda
1 ½ teaspoons baking powder
Pinch of salt
1 cup of milk

For frosting you will need:
1 cup of unsalted butter (can substitute cream cheese)
4 cups powdered sugar
½ cup of dark cocoa powder
2 teaspoons vanilla
4–5 tablespoons of milk

Preheat oven to 350 degrees.

In a large bowl mix butter, vanilla and sugar until light and fluffy. Add eggs and beat well. Put all dry ingredients in a large bowl. Mix lightly with a fork. Cupful by cupful sift back into the bowl until everything has been well sifted. Add to butter mixture, pausing to add milk in stages.

Divide into prepared, 9" round pans and bake for 23–30 minutes or until toothpick comes out clean from the center.

For the frosting pulse everything except the milk in a food processor until mostly blended. Add milk a tablespoon at a time until desired consistency is achieved.

Blackberry Buttermilk Cake with Sauternes

-gâteau de mûres au babeurre arrosé de Sauternes

This is it. This is your new cake, your dinner party *pièce de résistance*, and your new way to celebrate the first day of summer or congratulate a friend. If you can stop your family from nibbing all the blackberries off the top, then you are a better woman than I. It's constant hand slapping in our house until the cake is served. (We call stealing food, nibbing. Momma hollers, "No nibbing!" all the time around here!) The cake itself if so good that I now use it as the base for any of my yellow cake recipes. And don't panic, the directions call for a round, 9 inch pan but I use a heart shape now and again and you can too.

For the cake you will need:
2 cups of flour
1 teaspoon of baking powder
1 teaspoon of baking soda
¾ teaspoon of salt
½ cup unsalted butter
1 cup of sugar
1 teaspoon of bourbon vanilla
2 large eggs
1 cup well shaken buttermilk (You can simply add a little lemon juice to milk to make it sour if you don't have buttermilk on hand)

For the topping you will need:
¾ cup of Sauternes, Muscat or other dessert wine
4 tablespoons of sugar
2 tablespoon of grapefruit zest
⅓ cup of blackberry or other berry preserves
3–4 cups of fresh blackberries

Preheat the oven to 350 degrees. Line the bottom of a buttered 9 by 2 inch round pan with a round of wax paper. Butter the paper too.

Sift together the flour, baking powder, soda and salt. If you are new to baking/cooking this is a trick to delightful cakes that you won't want to leave out. Sift, sift, and sift. I don't have anything fancy just a wire/mesh strainer that I shake everything through.

Beat together the sugar and butter in a large bowl with an electric mixer until pale and fluffy then beat in the vanilla. Add the eggs one at a time, beating well after each. With your mixer on low, add the buttermilk until it is just combined. Add your sifted flour mixture in three batches, mixing after each until it is just combined.

Spoon the batter into your prepared cake pan, smoothing the top as best you can and bake it in the middle of the oven until golden and a tester comes out clean from the center. About 40–50 minutes. Cool the cake on a cake rack or cutting board and then run a knife around the edge and slide the cake onto a cake plate. If you find your cake has bulged and will not lay flat simply flip it over, bulge side up and take a serrated knife gently, horizontally through the cake, thus cutting of the bump. *Then eat it!!!!*

To make the topping:
Bring the wine, 3 tablespoons of sugar and grapefruit zest to a boil in a small saucepan, stirring until the sugar is dissolved and a syrup has been created. Boil until the syrup is reduced to about ⅔ of a cup. About 1–2 minutes.

Reserve 2 tablespoons of the syrup and pour the remainder slowly and evenly over the cake. Stir together the rest of the syrup, your preserves and remaining tablespoon of sugar in a small saucepan and simmer, stirring occasionally until thickened slightly, about 1 minute. It should be like think syrup. Put the blackberries in a large bowl, the pour preserves mixture over them.

Gently stir the berries with a rubber spatula to coat, and then pour over the cake! Serve warm if possible.

Pressed for time? The cake can be made a day ahead, fully cooled and wrapped in plastic wrap. The berry mixture is best made the day the cake is served.

Christmas Rum Cake

-gâteau de Noël au rhum

My Mom has been making this every year for Christmas for as long as I can remember. The Bundt shape and the hint of rum make this dessert festive but I have to say it's the moist, almost soggy pieces of cake that about do me in. Self-control? What's that? It goes flying out the window with this one. For holiday ease her recipe calls for a boxed yellow cake and instant vanilla pudding mix but I'm an ornery "from-scratch" kind of girl and so I use my yellow cake base (see page 199) and a homemade instant vanilla pudding mix.

If you're frantic with nativity plays and turkey basting the boxed cake and pudding mix still makes an absolutely wonderful cake. I'm proof of that, as I each as many pieces each year at Mom's as I can!

You will need:
Yellow cake as found on page 199, doubled or a boxed, yellow two-layer cake mix
1 ½ cups homemade, vanilla instant pudding or 14 ounces of boxed instant pudding
½ cup of dark rum
1 cup chopped pecans

Special equipment:
Bundt pan

For the instant pudding you will need:
3 cups of nonfat dry milk
4 cups of sugar
⅓ teaspoon of freshly grated nutmeg
3 cups of cornstarch
2 whole Bourbon vanilla beans

To make the glaze you will need:
1 cup of sugar
½ cup of butter
¼ cup of water
½ cup of dark rum

Preheat oven to 325 degrees.

To make the pudding mix combine all the ingredients except the vanilla bean. Slice the vanilla beans lengthwise and scrape out the insides. Mix the seedy paste in with the dry ingredients. Cut the remaining empty pods into quarters and mix them thoroughly in with everything else. Store in an airtight jar. For other recipes, know that one ½ cup equals a packet of instant mix.

To make the rum cake, make your yellow cake according to the directions on page 199. Evenly sprinkle the nuts onto the bottom of a greased Bundt pan. Combine the yellow cake mixture, the dry pudding mix and rum in a large mixer bowl and blend at medium speed for four minutes. Pour into the Bundt pan and bake at 325 degrees for about one hour or until a tester comes out clean. Do not under-bake. Cool in the pan and then invert onto a wire cooling wrack. Line newsprint underneath.

To make the glaze combine the water, butter and sugar in a small saucepan on medium-high heat until boiling. Boil for five minutes. Stir in the rum and bring it to where it just boils. Remove from heat.

Prick the bottom (flat side) of the cake with a skewer and pour some of the warm glaze into the holes of the cake. Turn the cake over and place onto it's serving tray and prick the top of the came and finish by pouring the remainder of the glaze into the cake.

French Style Hot Chocolate
-chocolat chaud

If you would ever like to have the city of Paris all to yourself, then head to bed early Saturday night and wake up early Sunday morning. To walk the streets of Paris early on a Sunday morning is to walk the most beautiful ghost town in the world. Normally bustling sidewalks are utterly empty and the boulevards are so barren that you can walk right out in the middle to snap a fabulous photograph. It is on Sunday mornings that we like to head out for croissants and hot chocolate. It's surprisingly quiet, the cafe chairs stacked high, one on top of the other as push brooms scuffle and mop water is tossed down in doorways. Late night revelers are stumbling home as you are just beginning to map out your day's adventures and what better way to do that than over a cup of *chocolat chaud*. While Angelina's in the Tuilleries gardens might be everyone's first choice for hot chocolate, ours is le Select, an old Hemingway haunt on the Boulevard Montparnasse. Rattan chairs, tile floors, crabby waiters and a resident cat make this café everything you need it to be. To top off your experience, sit facing the boulevard so you can watch the city ease to life as early morning fades away and be sure to order a cup of *chocolat chaud*.

You will need:
3.5 ounces of dark chocolate, 72% cacao recommended
1 cup of whole milk

Combine ingredients in a small saucepan and whisk over medium heat until blended. Top with Chantilly. Can be doubled, tripled, etc.

To Make a Pie

Simply put; a pie is a special thing. The pie is a tremendous part of our culinary American heritage. Pies are simple in that they almost always invoke a homespun, country feel, but the pie is nothing to scoff at. To make a perfect pie takes a certain skill, an enjoyment of one's kitchen and a desire to please those who will partake. There's a determination in rolling out the perfect crust and a tenderness as you crimp or detail the delicate edges. My Great Grandma was a farmgirl of great determination and tenderness. These are some of her pies and pies inspired by her.

The secret to Great Grandma's pie is her pie crust. I swear by it, though by the time the recipe was handed down to me it included shortening instead of lard. I imagine lard was the original ingredient before modern ways made her kitchen more "convenient."

Sometimes the old ways are the best.

Pie Crust
-pâte brisée américain

You will need:
3 cups flour
1 teaspoon of salt
1 cup of lard
1 egg, beaten
1 teaspoon of vinegar
5 tablespoons cold water

Mix together the flour, salt and lard. Add the egg, vinegar and cold water. Great Grandma used a pastry masher to get a super flaky crust and so do I. If you prefer an easier route you can mix in your food processor but you won't get the same results. If you use a food processor be sure to not over mix the pie dough.

This recipe makes enough for two 8–9 inch pies or enough for one pie with some left over for decorative crust details.

For a perfectly rolled pie crust use two clean dishtowels or flour sack towels. Place one on the counter top. Shape your dough into a ball and flatten it a bit with your hand to about an inch and a half thick. Lay the dough on the towel. Next, lay the second towel on top of the dough. Pull both towels to you so that they are hanging slightly over the counter top and use your stomach to hold them in place. This will keep them from getting away from you as you roll out your dough. Roll your dough to the desired size for your pie pan. The towels will prevent the dough from sticking to the counter top or your rolling pin. Remove the top towel and slide your hand under the bottom towel and pick up the crust and over turn it into your pie pan.

Cleaned counter space and cotton towels are as vital to successful construction as is a quality rolling pin. I have a couple marble rolling pins and I use them for my pies because they are heavy and do a great job moving the dough out. To successfully transfer your dough to the pie tin, roll it out onto a clean kitchen towel then simply slide your hand underneath and flip it into your tin, trimming off the excess or folding it over to crimp it.

Triple Berry Cream Pie
-tarte à la crème aux trois baies

Make your pie crust following the previous recipe. You can also follow this recipe and make an amazing peach pie or blueberry pie. The inspiration for this recipe comes from my second cousin Bev Bauer as found in our old, family cookbook.

You will need:
3–5 cups of fresh or frozen berries; blueberry, raspberry and blackberry blend (Be sure your berries or fruit are heaping because this pie settles and a high pie is a beautiful pie!)
2 eggs, beaten
1 ⅓ cup of sugar, divided, plus extra
1 cup flour, divided
½ cup of crème fraîche or sour cream in a pinch
½ cup of butter

Put half the berries in the pie shell. Preheat oven to 350.

In a separate bowl beat eggs and add 1 cup of the sugar, ½ of the flour and the crème fraîche. Mix thoroughly. Pour half the mixture over the berries, add the remaining berries and the rest of the mixture over the top.

Combine the remaining sugar, flour and butter and with a pastry masher or pulse with a food processor until pea sized crumble is formed. Sprinkle over the top and bake at 350 for just under an hour.

French Pressed Coffee

-and other fabulous coffee tips

This is hardly a recipe but more like a technique or rather, a *lifestyle*. French pressed coffee is, dare I say... real coffee. It's very easy but there are a couple professional tips to make the best pot of coffee you've ever had every single morning.

Begin with the whole bean coffee of your choice. I prefer an Italian or French roasted bean, which has a glossy or shiny surface and has dominant burned or charred notes with some brands having a hint of bittersweet. This is going to give you a more European taste than a Viennese or American bean.

Grind your beans to a large grain. (One tablespoon for two cups of coffee.) Not like sand or else it will escape through the press. I usually grind my beans for about eleven seconds. Too little grinding will make a thin, weak coffee. Too long and your coffee will be dirty.

Bring a pot of water to an almost boil. Pour the grounds into the French Press and add the water. Stir, cover with the lid but do not press.

In a few minutes gently press the palm of your hand on the press. If it begins to lower with ease that means the coffee grounds have settled and it is ready to press. If you feel resistance and it does not want to gently press, then you need to wait a few more minutes.

To keep your press warm you can wrap it with a small linen crossing the ends through the handle. Keep in mind that storing your coffee in the press while you enjoy the entire pot is going to increase the flavor of the coffee, possibly negatively.

Once your coffee is ready you may want to transfer it to a new carafe. If you choose to do this make additional hot water and fill the carafe with hot water while your coffee is being prepared.

Then empty the water before you add the coffee. This will give you a warm carafe in which to store your morning coffee.

Why not experiment with different flavors by adding fresh Chantilly to your coffee? You can also naturally change the flavor by adding dried lemon zest or cinnamon to your grounds.

Dutch Apple Pie

-tarte aux pommes néerlandaise

I've got family pie pride. Forget every apple pie you've ever eaten. This is Great Gramma's famous Dutch Apple and if you've been looking for the best apple pie ever, well, this is it. Actually, I have no right to say that, for this is just about the only apple pie I've ever had in my life and you'll soon see why. Be sure to save yourself a piece for breakfast the next morning. You'll thank me.

For the filling you will need:
8–12 Empire or McIntosh apples, peeled, cored and sliced
⅓ cup of flour
⅓ cup of sugar
4 tablespoons of ground cinnamon
(I prefer strong Saigon cinnamon)

For the topping:
½ cup of sugar
½ cup of flour
½ stick of butter

Follow basic pie crust recipe on page 204. In a large mixing bowl gently mix together the filling ingredients then pour the mixture into the prepared pie crust. The fruit should be heaping, as it will settle when baked.

With a pastry masher or with a food processor pulse the topping ingredients until a pea size crumble is formed. Sprinkle over the top and bake at 375 until bubbly and brown. About 45 minutes. Serve with quality vanilla ice cream.

About the author:

Angela J. Reed, Parisienne Farmgirl, lives with her husband and five children on a little "organique" farm near "Half-Way Farm" or *la ferme à mi-chemin* in the Midwest. Here they raise Nigerian Dwarf goats, chickens, rabbits and a variety of heirloom produce. On Half-Way Farm the family is learning the art of homesteading with the hopes of moving to a large farm someday soon where they can live completely off the land.

Angela makes her living as a leader with dōTERRA Essential Oils, and with a love of all things French and Farm she authors the blog, Parisienne Farmgirl, passionately writing about gardening, motherhood, France, homeschooling, fashion, health and farming with an amusing and Christian perspective.

For more Homesteading in High Heels you can follow Angela on social media. She is also available for speaking engagements when she's not working on her next cookbook...

At press time Angela was joyously expecting her sixth child.

Index of Recipes

16 Bean Soup 59
Ambrosia 135
Amélie's Honey Wheat Bread 179
Apple Ricotta Pancakes 182
Apples and Onions 70
Balsamic Vinaigrette 33
Basic Baguettes 174
Béchamel Sauce 42
Beef Stock 54
Blackberry Buttermilk Cake with Sauterne 199
Blue Cheese and Bean Potato Salad 68
Braised Leeks 77
Brambleberries with Simple Custard 190
Camembert with Pesto and Garlic 22
Cauliflower Gratin 80
Chamomile and Lavender French Toast 167
Chicken and Noodles 104
Chicken Stock 53
Childhood Chocolate Cake 198
Christmas Rum Cake 202
Cinnamon Rolls 168
Clarified Butter Sauce 36
Classic French Pancakes 172
Country Loaf 185
Cream of Wild Rice with Sage Soup 58
Crème Fraîche 115
Dinner Biscuits 171
Dressed Eggs 130
Dried Fruit and Chèvre 18
Dutch Apple Pie 208
Farm Style Green Beans 69
Feta Cheese 119
Flower Pepper 41
Foie Gras Mousse with Sauternes 21
French Onion Soup 62
French Pressed Coffee 207
French Style Hot Chocolate 203
Fried Potato Omelet 134
Garden Tacos 97
Gorgonzola Cream Sauce 42
Gramma's Strawberry Shortcake 192
Greek Yogurt 114

Green Onions and Salami 28
Half-Way Burger Buns 170
Half-Way Hamburgers 96
Herb Bouquet 152
Herbed Butter 158
Herbed Farm Potatoes, Two Ways 79
Homemade Brown Sugar 35
Homemade Kitchen Bouquet 43
Homemade Pasta 180
Hot Fudgy Pudding 197
Lavender Honey Butter 38
Leek and Potato Soup 61
Lemon and Oil Dressing 34
Mayonnaise 46
Mozzarella 128
Parisienne Pot Pie 100
Pasta Sauce 44
Peas -n- Cream 73
Perfectly Roasted Chicken 102
Pie Crust 204
Pizza Dough 173
Pork Loin with Herbs and Scallions 94
Pot Roast 90
Potager Pizza 7
Queen of Sheba Cake 194
Quiche 120
Red Onion Confit 39
Ricotta 127
Salt Crust Chicken with Rosemary 92
Shepherd's Pie 98
Shortcrust 162
Slaw Salad 66
Smoked Salmon Crêpes with Crème Fraîche 103
Sugared Egg 138
Summer Broccoli Salad 67
Summer Steak with Herb Butter 106
Sweet Carrots 87
Tapenade of Provence 32
The Cheese Plate 24
Tomato Vegetable Soup 56
Triple Berry Cream Pie 206

Made in the USA
Columbia, SC
16 October 2018